THE TOTAL SIMULATION OF MATRIMONIAL CONSENT

THE CATHOLIC UNIVERSITY OF AMERICA
CANON LAW STUDIES
No. 270

THE TOTAL SIMULATION OF MATRIMONIAL CONSENT

BY THE

REV. BASIL F. COURTEMANCHE, B.A., J.C.L.
PRIEST OF THE ARCHDIOCESE OF TORONTO

A DISSERTATION

SUBMITTED TO THE FACULTY OF THE SCHOOL OF CANON LAW OF THE CATHOLIC UNIVERSITY OF AMERICA IN PARTIAL FULFILLMENT OF THE REQUIREMENTS FOR THE DEGREE OF DOCTOR OF CANON LAW

THE CATHOLIC UNIVERSITY OF AMERICA
WASHINGTON, D.C.
1948

NIHIL OBSTAT:

LUDOVICUS MOTRY, S.T.D., J.C.D.,
Censor Deputatus

IMPRIMATUR:

✠JACOBUS C. CARDINAL MCGUIGAN, D.D.,
Archiepiscopus Torontinus,
Toronto, die 5 iunii, 1948.

PRINTED BY
THE MISSION PRESS
67 BOND STREET
TORONTO-CANADA

"Ecce ancilla Domini, fiat mihi secundum verbum tuum."

TO MARY, BRIDE OF THE HOLY SPIRIT

TABLE OF CONTENTS

FOREWORD

It is the doctrine of the Church that three elements must be present for a valid marriage, namely: the mutual consent of the parties, a legitimate manifestation of that consent, and the absence of any invalidating impediment.[1] That the present study is not concerned with the last of these elements is self-evident.

Whether between Christians or between unbaptized persons, marriage is essentially a contract.[2] The only difference between these two cases is that the marriage contract of two Christians is also a sacrament.[3] Though the sacramental nature of Christian marriage is very important, it does not pertain directly to the present study, which is concerned with the required consent for the matrimonial contract regardless of its sacramental or non-sacramental nature. It will be noted, however, that the question is not entirely irrelevant, inasmuch as the words or signs by which the consent is expressed are at the same time both the matter and the form of the sacrament. According as they signify the giving of the marital right they are the matter, and according as they signify the receiving of this right they constitute the form.[4]

In marriage, as in all contracts, there is a distinction between the matter, or the substance of the contract, and the

---

1 "Matrimonium facit partium consensus inter personas iure habiles legitime manifestatus; qui nulla humana potestate suppleri valet." —canon 1081, § 1.

2 The reference is to what theologians call *matrimonium in fieri*, and not to *matrimonium in facto esse*, that is, to the constitutive act of marriage, and not to marriage as an institution.

3 "Christus Dominus ad sacramenti dignitatem evexit ipsum contractum matrimonialem inter baptizatos."—canon 1012, § 1.

4 Sanchez, *Disputationum de Sancto Matrimonii Sacramento Tomi Tres* (3 vols., Venetiis, 1726), Lib. II, Disp. V, n. 6 (hereafter cited *De Matrimonio)*; Saurez, *Opera Omnia* (28 vols., Parisiis, 1856-1878), Vol. xx *De Sacramentis*, Quaest. LX, Art. VIII, Disp. II, Sect. I, p. 33; De Lugo, *Disputationes Scholasticae et Morales*, Vol. III, *Tractatus de Sacramentis in Genere* (Parisiis, 1868-1869), Disp. II, Sect. I, nn. 7-8; Schmalzgrueber, *Ius Ecclesiasticum Universum* (5 vols. in 12, Romae,

formalities which are required to effect the contract. The presence of the qualified witness or witnesses pertains to the formalities of the marriage contract, and hence to the legitimate manifestation of marital consent, which likewise is not directly pertinent to the present topic.

A marital consent may be defective because the person eliciting it was not capable of a rational consent, or because he was entirely ignorant of the nature of marriage, or again, because his consent was extorted under duress. All of these deficiencies of consent are also beyond the scope of the present study

The question at issue is that essential intrinsic defect of consent which is called *total simulation,* or simulation in the proper and strict sense. A person totally simulates matrimonial consent when he gives an apparent, external and serious manifestation of marital consent, but at the same time internally he positively intends not to marry. No abstruse concepts are involved in the substantial law concerning total simulation. Marriage can be effected only by the marital consent of both parties. But in the case of total simulation there is lacking a true consent on the part of one of the consorts. It is evident that a marriage to which one of the parties has totally simulated consent is null and void by the natural law.

The proof of the fact of simulation in a particular case is usually more complicated. The present study is an attempt to

---

1843-1845), Lib. IV, tit. I, n. 289; Gasparri, *Tractatus Canonicus de Matrimonio,* (ed. nova ad mentem Codicis I. C., 2 vols., Romae: Typis Polyglottis Vaticanis, 1932), I, n. 34 (hereafter cited *De Matrimonio);* Werns-Vidal, *Ius Canonicum* (7 vols. in 8, Romae: apud Aedes Universitatis Gregorianae, 1923-1938), Vol. V, *Ius Matrimoniale,* n. 43; De Smet, *Tractatus Theologico-Canonicus de Sponsalibus et Matrimonio* (ed. 4, Brugis: Car. Beyaert, 1927), n, 181 (hereafter cited *De Sponsalibus et Matrimonio);* Coronata, *Institutiones Iuris Canonici, Tractatus Canonicus de Sacramentis* (3 vols., Romae: Marietti, 1943-1946), III, n. 17 (hereafter cited *De Sacramentis);* Cappello, *Tractatus Canonico-Moralis de Sacramentis* (3 vols. in 6, Vol. III *De Matrimonio,* 4. ed., 1939, Romae: Marietti), III, n. 31 (hereafter cited *De Sacramentis);* Payen, *De Matrimonio in Missionibus ac Potissimum in Sinis Tractatus Practicus et Casus* (2. ed., 3 vols., Zi-ka-wei: in Typographia T'Ou-Se-We, 1935-1936), I, nn. 178-179 (hereafter cited *De Matrimonio).*

analyze the general mode of the procedure which is followed by the higher courts of the Church in adjudicating matrimonial cases of this type.

The author wishes to express his sincere thanks to His Eminence James C. Cardinal McGuigan, Archbishop of Toronto, for the opportunity of pursuing higher studies, to the members of the Faculty of the School of Canon Law for their generous direction and assistance, and to all others who have contributed towards the completion of this work.

TABLE OF CITED CASES

S. C. C., *Mutinen.*, 19 aug. 1724— *Codicis Iuris Canonici Fontes,* cura Emi Petri Card. Gasparri editi (9 vols., Romae postea Civitate Vaticana: Typis Polyglottis Vaticanis, 1923-1939, Vols. VII, VIII, IX ed. cura et studio Emi Iustiniani Card. Seredi), nn. 3282, 3299 (hereafter cited *Fontes); Thesaurus Resolutionum Sacrae Congregationis Concilii* (167 vols., Romae, 1718-1908), III, 66-68, 161-163 (hereafter cited *Thesaurus)*.

S. C. C., *Chien.*, 12 mart. 1729— *Fontes,* n. 3344 *Thesaurus,* IV, 267-271.

S. C. C., *Compostellana,* 19 aug. 1730— *Fontes,* n. 3363; *Thesaurus,* V. 37-39.

S. C. C., *Capuana seu Calven.*, 9 iul. 1757 — *Fontes,* n. 3674; *Thesaurus,* XXVI, 57.

S. C. C., *Pisana,* 2 maii 1868 — *Fontes,* n. 4211; *Thesaurus,* CXXVII, 288-300

S. C C., *Parisien.*, 7 iul., 1 sept. 1883— *Fontes,* n. 4259; *Thesaurus,* CXLII, 429-451.

Sacre Romanae Rotae Decisiones seu Sententiae quae iuxta Legem Propriam et Constitutionem "Sapienti Consilio" Pii PP. X. prodierunt, cura eiusdem S. Tribunalis editae (Romae, 1912—) II (1910), 19-32, Dec. III, coram R. P. D. Gustavo Persiani, 19 ian., — non constat (hereafter cited S. R. R.).

S. R. R., III (1911), 15-29, Dec. III, coram R. P. D. Seraphino Many, 24 ian., — constat.

S. R. R., III (1911), 236-244, Dec. XXII, coram R. P. D. Ioanne Prior, 9 iun., — constat.

S. R. R., III (1911), 325-331, Dec. XXIX, *Massilien.*, coram R. P. D. Guilelmo Sebastianelli, 1 iul., — constat.

S. R. R., III (1911), 346-352, Dec. XXXII, coram R. P. D. Ioanne Prior, 18 iul., — constat.

S. R. R., III (1911), 460-473, Dec. XL, coram Revmo Michaele Lega, Decano, 30 aug., — constat.

S. R. R., IV (1912), 401-408, Dec. XXXV, *Massilien.*, coram R. P. D. Ioanne Prior, 10 aug., — non constat.

S. R. R., IV (1912), 459-468, Dec. XL, coram R. P. D. Ioanne Prior, 13 dec., — non constat.

S. R. R., V (1913), 210-216, Dec. XVIII, coram R. P. D. Ioanne Prior, 8 mart., — constat.

S. R. R., VI (1914), 25-38, Dec. III, coram R. P. D. Iosepho Mori, 28 ian., — constat.

S. R. R., VI (1914), 244-253, Dec. XXII, *Oregonopolitana,* coram R. P. D. Ioanne Prior, 6 iul., — non constat.

S. R. R., VI (1914), 323-331, Dec. XXXI, coram R. P. D. Francisco Heiner, 28 nov., — non constat.

S. R. R., VII (1915), 194-206, Dec. XVIII, coram R. P. D. Antonio Perathoner, 21 apr., — constat.

S. R. R., VIII (1916), 48-58, Dec. IV, coram R. P. D. Seraphino Many, 29 febr., — non constat.

S. R. R., VIII (1916), 196-202, Dec. XVIII, coram, R. P. D. Seraphino Many, 16 iun., — non constat.

S. R. R., XI (1919), 36-45, Dec. IV, coram R. P. D. Ioanne Prior, 22 febr., — constat.

S. R. R., XII (1920), 46-54, Dec. VII *Parisien.,* coram R. P. D., Friderico Cattani Amadori, 10 mart., — non constat.

S. R. R., XII (1920), 63-70, Dec. IX, coram R. P. D. Maximo Massimi, 16 mart., — constat.

S. R. R., XIV (1922), 308-311, Dec. XXXIII, coram R. P. D. Maximo Massimi, 16 aug., — constat.

S. R. R., XV (1923), 21-38, Dec. IV, coram R. P. D. Friderico Cattani Amadori, 28 febr., — non constat.

S. R. R., V (1923), 142-147, Dec. XVI, coram R. P. D. Francisco Parrillo, 5 iul., — non constat.

S. R. R., XV (1923), 165-174, Dec. XIX, coram R. P. D. Francisco Parrillo, 18 iul., — non constat (but nullity was declared on the ground of the exclusion of the *bonum prolis).*

S. R. R., XVI (1924), 67-73, Dec. VIII, *Vic. Apost. Tonkini Marit.,* coram R. P. D. Andrea Jullien, 29 febr., — constat.

S. R. R., XVI (1924), 150-163, Dec. XIX, Colonien., coram R. P. D. Francisco Parrillo, 27 maii, — constat.

S. R. R., XVI (1924), 312-325, Dec. XXXVI, coram R .P. D. Andrea Jullien, 5 aug., — non constat.

S. R. R., XVII (1925), 47-61, Dec. VII, coram R. P. D. Andrea Jullien, 7 febr., — non constat.

S. R. R., XVII (1925), 173-182, Dec. XXIII, *Nicien.,* coram R. P. D. Ubaldo Mannucci, 28 apr., — non constat.

S. R. R., XVII (1925), 218-229, Dec. XXVIII, coram R. P. D. Francisco Morano, 6 iun., — non constat.

S. R. R., XVII (1925), 293-296, Dec. XXXVII, coram Rmo. P. D. Maximo Massimi, Pro-Decano, 27 iul., — constat.

S. R. R., VII (1925), 372-383, Dec. XLVI, coram R. P. D. Andrea Jullien, 13 nov., — non constat.

S. R. R., XVIII (1926), 33-42, Dec. VI, coram R. P. D. Iulio Grazioli, 13 febr., — constat.

S. R. R., XVIII (1926), 252-261, Dec. XXXII, coram R. P. D. Francisco Solieri, 26 iul., — constat.

S. R. R., XVIII (1926), 262-269, Dec. XXXIII, coram R. P. D. Francisco Parrillo, 28 iul., — non constat.

S. R. R., XIX (1927), 169-177, Dec. XXI, coram R. P. D. Iulio Grazioli, 10 maii, — non constat (dispensatio).

S. R. R., XIX (1927), 182-191, Dec. XXIII, coram R. P. D. Francisco Guglielmi, 28 maii, — non constat.

S. R. R., XIX (1927), 192-198, Dec. XXIV, coram R. P. D. Andrea Jullien, 1 iun., — non constat.

S. R. R., XIX (1927), 214-221, Dec. XXVII, coram R. P. D. Maximo Massimi, Decano, 8 iun., — constat.

S. R. R., XX (1928), 106-112, Dec. X, coram R. P. D. Francisco Parrillo, 4 apr., — non constat.

S. R. R., XX (1928), 245-249, Dec. XXVI, coram R. P. D. Ubaldo Mannucci, 16 iun., — non constat.

S. R. R., XX (1928), 342-346, Dec. XXXVII, *Vic. Apost. De Loango,* coram R. P. D., Iosepho Florczak, 31 iul., — constat.

S. R. R., XX (1928), 391-398, Dec. XLIV, coram Rmo. P. D. Maximo Massimi, Decano, 10 aug., — constat.

S. R. R., XXI (1929), 144-152, Dec. XVII, coram R. P. D. Francisco Guglielmi, 6 mart., — constat.

S. R. R., XXI (1929), 171-183, Dec. XXI, *Marianopolitana,* coram R. P. D. Francisco Guglielmi, 5 apr., — non constat (but nullity was declared on other grounds).

S. R. R., XXI (1929), 232-239, Dec. XXVII, *S. Hippolyti.,* coram R. P. D. Francisco Guglielmi, 28 iun., — constat.

S. R. R., XXI (1929), 259-268, Dec. XXXI, coram Rmo. P. D. Maximo Massimi, Decano, 9 iul., — non constat.

S. R. R., XXI (1929), 295-305, Dec. XXXV, coram R. P. D. Andrea Jullien, 17 iul., — non constat.

S. R. R., XXI (1929), 508-517, Dec. LXI, coram R. P. D. Francisco Parillo, 2 dec., — non constat.

S. R. R., XXI (1929), 530-538, Dec. LXIV, coram R. P. D. Maximo Massimi, Decano, 7 dec., — non constat.

S. R. R., XXI (1929), 547-553, Dec. LXVI, *Parisien.*, coram R. P. D. Henrico Quattrocolo, 17 dec., — non constat.

S. R. R., XXII (1930), 259-275, Dec. XXII, coram R. P. D. Francisco Parrillo, 10 maii, — non constat.

S. R. R., XXII (1930), 462-476, Dec. XLI, *Parisien.*, coram R. P. D. Arcturo Wynen, 26 iul., — non constat.

S. R. R., XXIII (1931), 57-67, Dec. VIII, *Algerien.*, coram R. P. D. Henrico Quattrocolo, 20 febr., — non constat.

S. R. R., XXIII (1931), 75-86, Dec. X, coram R. P. D. Henrico Quattrocolo, 3 mart., — constat.

S. R. R., XXIII (1931), 138-149, Dec. XVIII, *Constantinopolitana,* coram R. P. D. Arcturo Wynen, 18 apr., — non constat.

S. R. R., XXIII (1931), 194-202, Dec. XXIV, coram R. P. D., Henrico Quattrocolo, 2 iun., — non constat.

S. R. R., XXIII (1931), 224-235, Dec. XXVII, coram R. P. D. Arcturo Wynen, 16 iun., — non constat.

S. R. R., XXIII (1931), 292-304, Dec. XXXV, coram R. P. D. Francisco Guglielmi, 16 iul., — non constat.

S. R. R., XXIV (1932), 64-77, Dec. VIII, *Luganen.*, coram R. P. D. Iulio Grazioli, 16 febr., — constat.

S. R. R., XXIV (1932), 152-157, Dec. XVII, *Marianopolitana,* coram Exc. P. D. Maximo Massimi, Decano, 30 apr., — non constat (but nullity was declared on the ground of force and fear).

S. R. R., XXIV (1932), 207-212, Dec. XXII, *Katovicen,* coram R. P. D. Henrico Quattrocolo, 7 iun., — non constat.

S. R. R., XXV (1933), 25-37, Dec. IV, coram R. P. D. Francisco Guglielmi, 20 ian., — non constat.

S. R. R., XXV (1933), 77-86, Dec. X, coram R. P. D., Iulio Grazioli, 16 febr., — non constat.

S. R. R., XXV (1933), 241-252, Dec. XXVIII, *Lugdunen.*, coram R. P. D. Francisco Guglielmi, 21 apr., — non constat.

S. R. R., XXV (1933), 384-398, Dec. XLV, coram R. P. D. Francisco Guglielmi, 21 iun., — non constat.

S. R. R., XXV (1933), 442-449, Dec. LII, coram Excm. P. D. Maximo Massimi, Decano, 11 iul., — non constat.

S. R. R., XXV (1933), 450-456, Dec. LIII, coram R. P. D. Guillelmo Heard, 15 iul., — non constat.

S. R. R., XXV (1933), 461-479, Dec. LV, coram R. P. D. Iulio Grazioli, 17 iul., — non constat.

S. R. R., XXV (1933), 568-575, Dec. LXVII, *Magno Veradinen.*, coram R. P. D. Francisco Guglielmi, 14 nov., — non constat.

S. R. R., XXVI (1934), 1-11, Dec. I, *Angelorum et S. Didaci.*, coram R. P. D. Guillelmo Heard, 4 ian., — constat.

S. R. R., XXVI (1934), 71-79, Dec. VIII, *Meliten.*, coram R. P. D. Arcturo Wynen, 1 mart., — non constat.

S. R. R., XXVI (1934), 166-172, Dec. XVI, coram Excmo P. D. Maximo Massimi, Decano, 9 apr., — non constat.

S. R. R., XXVI (1934), 408-417, Dec. XLVI, *Reginaten.*, coram R. P. D. Henrico Quattrocolo, 19 iun., — non constat.

S. R. R., XXVI (1934), 450-456, Dec. LI, *Wratislavien.*, coram R. P. D. Francisco Morano, 26 iun., — non constat.

S. R. R., XXVI (1934), 465-473, Dec. LIV, *Liburnen.*, coram R. P. D. Iulio Grazioli, 2 iul., — constat.

S. R. R., XXVI (1934), 672-682, Dec. LXXIX, *Angelorum et S. Didaci.*, coram R. P. D. Francisco Guglielmi, 24 oct. — non constat.

S. R. R., XXVI (1934), 727-740, Dec. LXXXV, *Angelorum et S. Diadaci.*, coram R. P. D. Andrea Jullien, 10 nov., — non constat.

S. R. R., XXVII (1935), 332-343, Dec. XL, *Tergestina*, coram R. P. D. Iulio Grazioli, 27 maii, — non constat.

S. R. R., XXVII (1935), 519-530, Dec. LXI, *Parisien.*, coram R. P. D. Arcturo Wynen, 3 aug., — constat.

S. R. R., XXVII (1935), 542-550, Dec. LXIV, *Ianuen.*, coram R. P. D. Guillelmo Heard, 8 aug., — non constat.

S. R. R., XXVII (1935), 551-556, Dec. LXV, *Calaritana*, coram R. P. D. Arcturo Wynen, 8 aug., — non constat.

S. R. R., XXVII (1935), 620-631, Dec. LXXIV, *Tarentina*, coram R. P. D. Iulio Grazioli, 2 dec., — non constat.

S. R. R., XXVII (1935), 703-708, Dec. LXXXIV, coram R. P. D. Andrea Jullien, 23 dec., — non constat.

S. R. R., XXVIII (1936), 99-114, Dec. XI, *Matriten.*, coram R. P. D. Arcturo Wynen, 6 febr., — non constat.

S. R. R., XXVIII (1936), 129-135, Dec. XIII, coram R. P. D. Guillelmo Heard, 15 febr., — non constat.

S. R. R., XXVIII (1936), 303-319, Dec. XXXIII, *Florentina*, coram R. P. D. Andrea Jullien, 9 maii, — non constat.

S. R. R., XXVIII (1936), 602-619, Dec. LXIV, coram R. P. D. Henrico Quattrocolo, 17 oct., — non constat.

S. R. R., XXIX (1937), 69-76, Dec. IX, *Ianuen.*, coram R. P. D. Ioanne Teodori, 9 febr., — non constat.

S. R. R., XXIX (1937), 98-109, Dec. XII, *Vilnen.*, coram R. P. D. Arcturo Wynen, 18 febr., — constat.

S. R. R., XXIX (1937), 148-157, Dec. XV, coram R. P. D. Henrico Quattrocolo, 25 febr., — non constat.

S. R. R., XXIX (1937), 314-318, Dec. XXX, *Varsavien.*, coram R. P. D. Arcturo Wynen, 29 apr., — non constat.

S. R. R., XXIX (1937), 525-538, Dec. LIII, coram R. P. D. Alberto Canestri, 15 iul., — non constat.

S. R. R., XXIX (1937), 556-567, Dec. LVI, *Parisien.*, coram Exc.mo P. D. Iulio Grazioli, Decano, 30 iul., — constat.

S. R. R., XXIX (1937), 663-674, Dec. LXVII, *Ianuen.*, coram R. P. D. Andrea Jullien, 13 nov., — non constat.

S. R. R., XXIX (1937), 674-684, Dec. LXVIII, *Rapidopolitana,* coram R. P. D. Henrico Quattrocolo, 16 nov., — constat.

S. R. R., XXIX (1937), 733-740, Dec. LXXIV, *Czestochovien.*, coram R. P. D. Andrea Jullien, 11 dec., — non constat.

S. R. R., XXX (1938), 343-350, Dec. XXXVIII; *Vindobonen.*, coram R. P. D. Andrea Jullien, 23 iun., — non constat.

S. R. R., XXX (1938), 369-381, Dec. XLI, coram Exc.mo P. D. Iulio Grazioli, Decano, 30 iun., — non constat (but nullity was declared on the ground of force and fear).

S. R. R., XXX (1938), 585-591, Dec. LXV, *Jaurinen.*,- coram R. P. D. Ioanne Teodori, 12 nov., — non constat.

S. R. R., XXX (1938), 640-646, Dec. LXX, *Romana,* coram R. P. D. Henrico Quattrocolo, 30 nov., — non constat.

From 1939 to 1946 inclusive, the Rota gave decisions in 597 nullity cases, in 32 of which marriage was impugned on the ground of total simulation. Of these, 27 were cases that had been brought before the Rota for their initial hearing.

In addition to the cases listed above the present study contains references to the following cases:

S. R. R., III (1911), 332-340, Dec. XXX, coram R. P. D. Francisco Heiner, 7 iul., — force and fear, — constat.

S. R. R., V (1913), 242-248, Dec. XXI, *Ce-li Merido-Occidentalis,* coram R. P. D. Francisco Heiner, 16 apr., — deficient consent and error, — constat.

S. R. R., V (1913), 283-292, Dec. XXV, *Vicariatus Apostolici Nova Pomeraniae,* coram R. P. D. Seraphino Many, 30 apr., — deficient consent, — constat.

S. R. R., XV (1923), 21-38, Dec. IV, coram R. P. D. Friderico Amadori, 28 febr., — threefold partial simulation, — non constat.

S. R. R., XV (1923), 198-202, Dec. XXVI, coram R. P. D. Maximo Massimi, 6 aug., — exclusion of the *bonum sacramenti,* — constat.

S. R. R., XVII (1925), 67-73, Dec. IX, *Posnanien.,* coram R. P. D. Andrea Jullien, 11 febr., — force and fear, — constat.

S. R. R., XIX (1927), 466-472, Dec. LII, *Varsavien.,* coram Exc.mo P. D. Maximo Massimi, Decano, 24 nov., — deficient consent and force and fear, — nullity was declared on ground of force and fear.

S. R. R., XX (1928), 442-450, Dec. LI,*Varmien.,* coram R. P. D. Iulio Grazioli, 25 oct., — deficient consent, — non constat.

S. R. R., XXI (1929), 206-217, Dec. XXV, *Parisien.,* coram R. P. D. Andrea Jullien, 5 iun., — exclusion of the *bonum sacramenti,* — non constat.

S. R. R., XXI (1929), 425-433, Dec. LI, coram R. P. D. Ubaldo Mannucci, 10 aug., — exclusion of the *bonum prolis* and the *bonum sacramenti,* — non constat.

S. R. R., XXII (1930), 191-201, Dec. XVI, *Paderbornen.,* coram R. P. D. Henrico Quattrocolo, 2 apr., — exclusion of the *bonum sacramenti.,* — non constat.

S. R. R., XXII (1930), 384-392, Dec. XXXIV, coram R. P. D. Andrea Jullien, 9 iul., — exclusion of the *bonum sacramenti,* — non constat.

S. R. R., XXIII (1931), 286-292, Dec. XXXIV, *Nicien.,* coram R. P. D. Henrico Quattrocolo, 16 iul., — exclusion of the *bonum prolis* and the *bonum sacramenti,* — non constat.

S. R. R., XXIV (1932), 107-115, Dec. XII, *Leodien.,* coram R. P. D. Iulio Grazioli, 18 mart., — exclusion of the *bonum sacramenti,* — non constat.

S. R. R., XXIV (1932), 482-492, Dec. LII, *Katovicen.,* coram R. P. D. Francisco Morano, 6 dec., — deficient consent (lack of manifestation), — non constat.

S. R. R., XXVIII (1936), 1-13, Dec. I, *Parisien.,* coram R. P. D. Andrea Jullien, 16 ian., — deficient consent, — non constat.

CHAPTER I

THE DOCTRINE OF TOTAL SIMULATION OF CONSENT PRIOR TO THE COUNCIL OF TRENT

From the beginning of its history, the Church has taught at least implicitly that the element of consent is essential to matrimony.[1]

[1]To prove conclusively the truth of this statement would be beyond the scope of the present work, and thus the following texts are cited merely as examples of the constant tradition: St. Ambrose, *De Institutione Virginis*, Liber I, Cap VI; ". . .non enim defloratio virginitatis facit conjugium sed pactio conjugalis. Denique cum jungitur puella, conjugium est, non cum virili admixtione cognoscitur."—Migne, *Patrologiae Cursus Completus, Series Latina* (221 vols., Parisiis, 1844-1864), XVI, 316 (hereafter this work will be referred to as *MPL)*; St. Augustine, *De Nuptiis et Concupiscentia*, Lib. I, Cap. XI; "Conjux vocatur ex prima desponsationis fide, quam concubitu nec cognoverat, nec fuerat cogniturus: nec perierat, nec mendax manserat appellatio, ubi fuerat carnis ulla commixtio."—*MPL*, XLIV, 420. This text is also found in the *Corpus Scriptorum Ecclesiasticorum Latinorum* (editum consilio et impensis Academiae Litterarum Caesareae Vindobonensis, 71 vols., Pragae, Vindobonae, Lipsiae, 1866-), XLII, 224 (hereafter this work will be cited as *CSEL)*. cf. also St. John Chrysostom, *Opus Imperfectum in Evangelium Matthaei*, Homil. XXXII: "Matrimonium non facit coitus sed voluntas."—Migne, Patrologiae Cursus completus Series Graeca (161 vols., Parisiis, 1856-1866), LVI, 802; Hugh of St. Victor, *Quaestiones et Decisiones in Epistolas D. Paulis in Epistolam Primam ad Corinthios*, Quaest. LVI: "Causa efficiens est consensus materialis per verba de praesenti expressus. Consensus qui in anima est, debet demonstrari, sine quo non est coniugium, unde legitur, 'Matrimonium non facit copula corporum, sed voluntas animarum.' "—*MPL*, CLXXV, 524; Pope St. Nicholas I (Reply of the year 866 to the Christians of Bulgaria): "Sufficiat secundum leges solus eorum consensus, de quorum coniunctionibus agitur; qui consensus, si solus in nuptiis forte defuerit, cetera omnia, etiam cum ipso coitu celebrata, frustrantur."—Denzinger—Bannwart—Umberg, *Enchiridion Symbolorum Definitionum et Declarationum de Rebus Fidei et Morum* (21.-23. ed., Friburgi Brisgoviae, St. Louis: Herder, 1937), n. 334 (hereafter cited Denziger); Jaffé, *Regesta Pontificum Romanorum ab condita Ecclesia ad annum post Christum natum MCXCVIII* (2. ed., 2 vols., Lipsiae, 1885-1888), Vol. I, n. 2812; Pope Innocent III, letter to the bishop of Modena (1200): "In matrimoniis de cetero contrahendis illud te volumus observare, ut, postquam inter personas legitimas consensus mutuus intervenerit de praesenti, qui sufficit in talibus iuxta canonicas sanctiones, et si personae iunctae legitime cum aliis postea de facto contrahant, quod prius de iure factum fuerit, non poterit irritari."—Denzinger, n. 404; Potthast, *Regesta Pontificum Romanorum inde ab anno post Christum natum MCXCVIII ad annum MCCCIV* (2 vols., Berolini, 1874-1875), Vol. I, n. 1238. (This text is also found in c. 5, X, *de sponsa duorum*, IV, 4). Council of Florence (1439-1445): "Causa efficiens matrimonii regulariter est mutuus

However, in spite of the universality of this recognition, no direct reference to simulated consent is found in the canonical sources previous to the twelfth century. It was only with Alexander III (1159-1181) that consent was officially recognized as the sole efficient cause of matrimony, and only thereafter did canonists begin to analyze fully its many implications.[2]

With marriage considered as a contract, and again as a sacrament, it is evident that both internal consent and the external manifestation thereof are necessary for validity. These are the words of St. Thomas:

> In matrimony there is a contract between husband and wife. Now in every contract there must be expression of the words by which men bind themselves mutually to one another. Therefore in matrimony also the consent must be expressed in words.
>
> Matrimony is a sacrament. Now a sensible sign is required in every sacrament. Therefore it is also required in matrimony, and consequently there must needs be at least words by which the consent is made perceptible to the senses.[3]

Peter Lombard (c. 1100-1160.)[4] seems to have been the first to consider the effects of a feigned matrimonial consent. After distinguishing between *"consensus de futuro"* and *consensus de praesenti,"* and stating that only the latter is the efficient cause of matrimony, he continued in the following words:

> If they internally consent but do not express their consent by words or other certain signs, such a consent does not

consensus per verba de praesenti expressus."—Mansi, *Sacrorum Conciliorum Nova et Amplissima Collectio* (53 vols. in 60, Paris-Arnhem-Leipsig, 1901-1927), XXXI, 1058 (hereafter cited as Mansi); Council of Trent, Sess. XXIV, *de ref. matrim.*, cap. 1. The doctrine is mentioned in the "*Tametsi*" decree.

[2]Cf. c. 6, *de sponsa duorum et e converso*, IV, 1, in Compilatio I—Friedberg, *Quinque Compilationes Antiquae* (Lipsiae: 1882).

[3]*Summa Theologica*, Pars III, Suppl., q. 45, art. 2. The English version is from *The Summa Theologica* of Saint Thomas Aquinas literally translated by the Fathers of the English Dominican Province (22 vols., Burns-Oates and Washbourne, Ltd., 1912-1936), XIX, pp. 115-116.

[4]Cf. McSorley, *An Outline History of the Church by Centuries* (St. Louis: Herder, 1945), p. 354.

effect matrimony. If, on the other hand, they express by words what they do not will in their hearts, and if there is no question of force or fraud, that obligation of the words by which they consent, . . . effects marriage.[5]

Later canonists emphasized and clarified the fact that this statement has the force only of a presumption in the external form.

In the year 1212 a case in which fraud had been exercised was submitted to Pope Innocent III (1198-1216). The response of the Pontiff comprises the first pontifical document dealing directly with simulated matrimonial consent. This, the famous Decretal "*Tua nos,*" was included in the *Compilatio* IV,[6] and later incorpoated in the Decretals of Gregory IX.

A certain man, being unable to seduce a woman because of her insistence that he espouse her before she would surrender her person, spoke to her the following words without any solemnity and in the absence of any witnesses: "John marries you." He did not believe that he was really married, for John was not his name, and he had an intention, not of contracting marriage, but simply of having carnal relations with the woman. The Pope was asked whether this was a true marriage. The man had indeed not given a true consent, but the woman had done so, and carnal relations had followed. The Pope replied that in view of the fact that the man, in his own person, espoused *(desponsaverit)* the woman even though under a pretended name, and in consideration of the subsequent carnal relations, it would seem that the decision possibly should be in favor of the validity of the union. But, if what had been alleged was true, namely, that the man did not in-

[5]Lib. V, Dist. XXVII, Cap. 3: "Efficiens autem causa matrimonii est consensus, non quilibet, sed per verba expressus, nec de futuro sed de praesenti. Si enim consentiunt in futurum, dicentes: Accipiam te in virum, et ego te in uxorem; non iste consensus est efficax matrimonii. Item, si consentiant mente, et non exprimant verbis vel aliis certis signis, nec talis consensus efficit matrimonium. Si autem verbis explicatur quod tamen corde non volunt; si non sit ibi coactio vel dolus, obligatio illa verborum, quibus consentiunt dicentes: Accipio te in virum, et ego te in uxorem, matrimonium facit"—*Petri Lombardi Sententiarum Libri Quattuor* (ed. Migne, Paris, 1853), c. 400.

[6]C. 1, *de sponsalibus et matrimoniis*, IV, 1.

tend to marry the woman, and thus did not give marital consent, then the decision was otherwise, though the Pope confessed that he did not see how that fact was definitely known. However, he was undertaking simply to state the law, for if the case corresponded in fact to the report, that is, if the man did not intend to take the woman as his wife, and at no time gave consent, then the union could not be judged a true marriage, since there was not to be found in it the substance of the conjugal contract, inasmuch as on the one side there was only deceit, and no presence of consent. In the absence of consent nothing else could produce the bond.[7]

The Decretal thus presented an evident case of simulated matrimonial consent. The man, having no intention of marrying the woman, feigned consent, in order that he might attain his immoral purpose.

It is to be noted that the Pope did not consider the marriage invalid simply for the reason that the man made use of a fictitious name. Words are to be considered as furnishing a manifestation of what is in the mind. Words in themselves do not effect marriage except in so far as they manifest the presence of an internal consent. In the case proposed it was

---

[7] "Tua nos duxit fraternitas consulendos. . .quaesivisti ut quum quandam mulierem quidam aliter inducere nequivisset ut sibi commisceretur carnaliter, nisi desponsasset eandem, nulla solemnitate adhibita vel alicuius praesentia, dixit illi: 'te Ioannes desponsat,' quum ipse Ioannes non vocaretur, se finxit se vocari Ioannem, non credens esse coniugium eo, quod ipse non vocaretur hoc nomine, nec haberet propositum contrahendi, sed copulam tantum exsequendi carnalem, utrum inter praedictos sit matrimonium celebratum, quum mulier consenserit et consentiat in eundem et ille dissenserit et dissentiat, nec aliud quicquam egerit, quam superius est expressum, nisi quod cognoverit eandem. Super quod tibi respondemus, quod, quum praefatus vir praedictam desponsaverit mulierem in propria persona et sub nomine alieno, quo tunc vocari se finxit et inter eos sit carnalis copula subsecuta, videtur forte pro coniugio praesumendum, nisi tu nobis expresse scripsisses, quod ille nec proposuit, nec consentit illa ducere in uxorem, quod qualiter tibi constiterit non videmus. Nos autem, quid iuris sit rescribentes, hoc dicimus, quod si res ita se habuerit, videlicet, quod ille eam non proposuit ducere in uxorem, nec unquam consensit in praedictam personam, non debet ex illo facto coniugium iudicari, quum in eo nec substantia coniugalis contractus, nec etiam forma contrahendi coniugium valeat inveniri, quoniam ex altera parte dolus solummodo adfuit, et defuit omnino consensus, sine quo cetera nequeunt foedus perficere coniugale." —c. 26, X, *de sponsalibus et matrimoniis*, IV, 1.

apparent from the circumstances, especially from the fact of the subsequent carnal relations, that the man, despite his use of another's name, was in reality referring to himself. Hence the statement of the Pope:

> . . . . quum praefatus vir praedictam desponsaverit mulierem in propria persona et sub nomine alieno, quo tunc vocari se finxit, et inter eos sit carnalis copula subsecuta, videtur forte pro coniugio praesumendum.

Nevertheless he declared that, as long as what had been alleged was true, namely, that the man did not intend to marry the woman (*"nisi tu nobis expresse scripsisses . . . . etc."*), then the marriage was invalid, and precisely so because on the part of the man the element of consent was lacking*("quoniam ex altera parte dolus solummodo adfuit et defuit omnino consensus.")*.

It was indeed unclear to the Pope in just what manner that assertion could be substantiated (*"quod qualiter tibi constiterit non videmus."*). Yet he accepted the statement of the bishop as fact; he himself simply applied the principle of the law, *("Nos autem quid iuris sit rescribentes")*

This reply of Innocent III was included in the Gregorian Decretals, and became the norm and the basis upon which all later canonists constructed their doctrine regarding simulated consent.

The *Compilatio* IV, in which Innocent's Decretal was first incorporated, appeared about the years 1216 - 1217.[8] During the third decade of the thirteenth century, St. Raymond of Pennafort (+1275) wrote the first three parts of his *Summa de Casibus.* The fourth part, which treats of marriage, was composed only about 1235-1236, and was based on the *Summa de Matrimonio* of Tancred (+1234-1236), which had been written about the same time as the Decretal itself (1210-1214).[9]

---

[8]Van Hove, *Commentarium Lovaniense in Codicem Iuris Canonici,* Vol. I, Tom. I, *Prolegomena ad Codicem Iuris Canonici* (ed. altera auctior et emendatior, Mechliniae-Romae: H. Dessain, 1945), p. 448 (hereafter cited as *Prolegomena).*

[9]Van Hove, *Prolegomena,* p. 451, and p. 513.

Actually St. Raymond added nothing new to the obvious meaning of the Decretal. He furnished the same example, that of a man who without the intention of contracting marriage had, for outward appearances, espoused a woman, but in inner purpose looked to the gaining of carnal pleasure. In response to the query whether such a procedure constituted the contracting of matrimony, he rendered a negative answer, for, as he explained, the substance of the conjugal contract was lacking. He concluded his argument with an appeal to the Decretal of Innocent III.[10]

So also in his treatment of the necessity of internal consent, St. Thomas maintained that the external sign of consent effects nothing, unless this external sign is in fact a true manifestation of what is in the mind. He, too, cited the Decretal of Innocent III.[11]

Although the Decretal *"Tua nos"* became the basis of all subsequent canonical teaching on the subject of feigned matrimonial consent, that teaching was not by any means uniform. The interpretation of the Decretal, as it was given above, has become the one which is universally held today. According to that interpretation, the Pope's decision looked simply to the external forum, for which he desired to state the law. Objectively a marriage was invalid whenever consent for it was lacking, and the nullity of such a union could be declared in the external forum. Yet the presumption of validity was so strong that proof to the contrary could be acknowledged only with great precaution. It was evident that the Pontiff did not propose to set up any norms for the evaluation of that proof. With reference to the proposed case, many of the decretalists could not envision how it was possible to establish that proof in the external forum. Accordingly their effort to stand by the strong presumption which favored the

---

[10]Sanctus Raymundus de Pennafort, *Summa* (Verone, 1744), lib. IV, tit. II, n. 2: "In hoc casu diversi diversa sentiunt; mihi tamen videtur, salvo meliore judicio, quod si ille non proposuit eam ducere in uxorem, nec unquam consensit in eam, non debet ex illo facto matrimonium judicari, quum in eo substantia conjugalis contractus non valeat inveniri."

[11]*Summa Theologica*, Pars III, Suppl., q. 45, art. 4, *sed contra*.

validity of marriage led them to strained interpretations of Innocent's Decretal.[12]

In his *Summa,* which was written about 1250-1253,[13] Hostiensis (+1271) was very reluctant to admit the nullity of the marriage case proposed in the Decretal. By way of general rule he upheld the validity of such a marriage. The reasons he assigned for his stand were the very ones that are used at the present time in support of the validity of a contested marriage, namely, that the words were to be understood in their ordinary meaning; that the unsupported assertion of one who impugned the marriage was to be rejected; that as long as any doubt persisted the marriage was to be considered valid.[14]

It seems that only when the words were spoken in an obviously joking manner did Hostiensis hold for the nullity of the marriage in question. In such an event he recommended recourse to the Pope as in major and difficult cases. He then suggested the following rule as applicable: If both parties under oath admitted that they had the intention of contracting marriage, then their deposition should be accepted as conclusively pointing to the existence of a valid contract. If only one of the parties claimed the presence of an intention to contract marriage, then the union should be adjudged as presumptively valid. Hostiensis felt that the Pope could well decide in favor of the validity of such a marriage, and he alleged as a basis for this rule the safeguarding of due respect for the sacramental character attaching to Christian marriage.[15]

12Cf. Esmein, *Le Mariage en Droit Canonique* (2 vols., Vol 1, deuxieme edition mise à jour par R. Génestal, Paris: Librairie du Recueil Sirey, 1929), I, 339.

13Van Hove, *Prolegomena,* p. 476.

14Hostiensis (Henricus de Segusio), *Summa Aurea* (Lugduni: 1568), IV, tit. I, cap. 2, n. 11: "Quid si taliter dicat se verba ludendi animo protulisse, videtur quod sit pro matrimonio judicandum; tum quia ad communem intellectum recurrendum est, nec ejus simplici assertioni credendum est qui matrimonium contradicit; tum quia in dubio semper est pro matrimonio judicandum; tum quod tutius et certius est, maxime respectu animae, interpretandum est, et ut res magis valeat quam pereat."

15*Summa Aurea,* Lib. IV, tit. I, cap. 2, n. 12: "Sed si ambo confiteantur quod intendebant contrahere, standum est confessioni eorum. . . Sin

Bernard of Parma died in 1266. Towards the end of his life he completed his *Gloss* on the Decretals of Gregory IX.[16] The Gloss to the Decretal in question admitted that a marriage could be null on the ground of simulated consent, "*quia simulatae nuptiae non sunt nuptiae.*"[17]

Yet Bernard also declared that a marriage which had been contracted publicly should not be declared invalid, even though one of the parties protested that prior to the marriage he had stated his lack of intention to contract matrimony. In such a case, according to Bernard, the Church was to judge in favor of the validity of the marriage by ignoring the protest which militated against it.[18]

In his treatment, of the latter portion of the Decretal, Bernard added a note to the effect that in view of the subsequent carnal relations between the two parties it was to be presumed that the man had consented to marriage. [19]

As with Hostiensis, so with Bernard of Parma, the reasons asserted for his doctrine were legally sound. Bernard claimed that the words as expressed were understood in their common signification, and certainly the expressed words of consent did

---

autem alter negat, alter confiteatur, bene faceret Papa si jus constitueret quod matrimonium teneret in poenam illius qui clandestine contraxit et qui forte modo poenitet. Unde ad instantiam illius non videtur matrimonium separandum. . .Nec enim debent laici de sacramentis Ecclesiae ludum facere vel derisum, et sic in dubio judicare."

[16]Van Hove, *Prolegomena*, p. 473; S. Kuttner, "The '*Glossa Ordinaria*' to the Gregorian Decretals"—*The English Historical Review* (London Longmans, Green and Co., 1886—), LX (1945), 97-105.

[17]C. 26, X, IV, 1, ad v. *mulierem.*

[18]*Loc. cit.*: "Sed pone quod aliquis protestetur coram pluribus, quod omnia quae dicet vel faciet, non faciet animo contrahendi matrimonio, et postea publice dicat, 'consentio in te': numquid est hic matrimonium vel non? In casu isto dico quod Ecclesia debet judicare pro matrimonio: quia recurrendum est ad communem verborum intelligentiam. Talia enim verba non possunt servire suae intentioni. Praeterea si probet quod illa verba protestatus fuit primo, potuit postea recedere ab illa voluntate, et consentire in illam, et hoc videtur per illud quod postea publice facit; et si dicat quod adhuc tempore contractus erat in eadem voluntate, non creditur ei: quia contra eum debet fieri interpretatio qui dolum adhibet." In support of the same view a quotation of Joannes Andreae (+1348) was inserted by a later glossator: "....et recte, nam aliter daretur omnibus matrimonia contrahentibus materia sic protestandi ut postea diverterent a conjugibus si displiceret."

[19]*Ibid.*, ad v. *Copula subsecuta.*

not signify a retention of that consent. Moreover, even if the fact of a previous contrary statement were conclusively established, the possibility of a change of heart for the giving of a subsequent consent was not thereby eliminated, especially when the words of consent were spoken publicly. Thus the presumption stood for the validity of the marriage, so that the interpretation of the facts militated in disfavor of the party who had played a deceiving role.

Some years after the appearance of the *Gloss* of Bernard of Parma, Hostiensis produced his second work, the *Commentaria*.[20] When he referred in this work to the doctrine proposed by Bernard, he took exception to a statement made by the glossator. Whereas Bernard had denied all probative value to a party's confession of simulation when the marriage was contracted publicly, Hostiensis claimed that such a protestation should be accepted in the external forum, provided that a reasonable cause was advanced in explanation of the act of simulation. According to Hostiensis, the factor of fear, for example, could underlie such a reasonable cause. But even the presence of duress or fear was of no consequence in substantiating the alleged act of simulation in the event that carnal relations had followed, for Hostensis, like Bernard, regarded that fact as connoting the giving of previous matrimonial consent.[21]

In an effort to harmonize the papal legislation with the juridic practice of the day, Hostiensis advanced the theory that only the first part of the Decretal, that is, up to the words "*Nos autem*," had any relation to the external forum, and that the second part indicated the norm applicable for the forum of conscience.[22] According to this interpretation, Pope Innocent III in the first part of the Decretal actually decided in favor of the validity of the marriage in the external forum, whereas in the second part, in which the nullity of the marriage was acknowledged, he disposed of the matter simply for the

[20]Van Hove, *Prolegomena*, p. 478.

[21]Hostiensis, *Commentaria in Quinque Decretalium Libros* (5 vols. in 3, Venetiis, 1581), Lib. IV, tit. I, cap. 26, n. 6 (hereafter cited *Commentaria).*

[22]*Commentaria*, Lib. IV, tit. I, cap. 26, n. 1-6.

internal forum. This interpretation was well received at the time, and many of the later decretalists followed it.

The *Apparatus* to the *Summa* of St. Raymond of Pennafort,[23] at the chapter in question, mentioned the opinion of Hostiensis which distinguished between the two fora, but differed with it. According to the *Apparatus,* if the words of consent were spoken in the normal manner, that is, "*de praesenti,*" then, even though in the subsequent act of carnal relations the party had simply an intention of fornicating, the marriage was nevertheless considered valid in both fora, so that proof to the contrary was inadmissible. However, if the consent was expressed with words similar to the form mentioned in the Decretal ("John marries you"), then the presumption of validity could yield to contrary proof through which the presence of fraud was conclusively established; yet the furnishing of such proof was a very difficult matter to procure. Once procured, however, the nullity of the marriage could be pronounced for the external forum as well.[24] This was the doctrine that eventually was to triumph over the other proposed opinions.

Henricus Bohic (+1350), writing almost a century after Hostiensis,[25] agreed with the latter's teaching regarding the application of Innocent's Decretal and the fact that there had to be a reasonable cause in evidence if the party's confession of simulation was to prove acceptable in the external forum.[26] Following the *Gloss* as well as Hostiensis, he likewise maintained that even with the presence of a just cause for the simulation conclusively established, the party's protestation of a simulated consent remained without juridical efficacy as a means of proof if an act of carnal relations had followed, so that the union stood presumptively recognized as valid.

[23] This *Apparatus* was begun by William of Rennes about the years 1241-1250, and enlarged by John of Freiburg (+1314) at a later date (1280-1298). The edition of St. Raymond's *Summa* which is available to the writer does not contain the complete *Apparatus*. It offers only certain passages without indicating individual authorship. Cf. Van Hove, *Prolegomena*, p. 514.

[24] *Apparatus* to the Summa of St. Raymond, Lib. IV, tit. 2, n. 2.

[25] Van Hove, *Prolegomena*, p. 495.

[26] *In Quinque Decretalium Libros Commentaria* (Venetiis, 1576), Lib. IV, tit. I, cap. 26, nn. 4-5.

Bohic also referred to certain writers, including Petrus de Sampsona, a professor at the School of Bologna in the thirteenth century,[27] but he differed with their opinion. These writers apparently held that the protestation should be accepted if the confession regarding the simulated consent had been made immediately before the manifestation of apparent consent.

Finally, Bohic formulated a principle that has survived until the present day as a norm in the evaluation of proof, namely, that if there was an interval of time between the marriage and the protestation regarding the lack of consent (the confession), then less credence was to be given to such a protestation than when it was made immediately after the marriage ceremony.

Nicholas de Tudeschis (Abbas Panormitanus), who flourished in the first half of the fifteenth century, in his excellent commentary on the Decretals, followed the doctrine of Hostiensis in this matter. He, too, claimed that, up to the words, "*Nos autem,*" the Decretal dealt with the matter having reference to the external forum. With regard to this he explained: *in quo quis non auditur allegans turpitudinem suam.*"[28] He also argued for the presumptive validity of the marriage when an act of carnal relations had followed for "*dolus non debet sibi prodesse, nam interpretatio fieri debet contra dolosum, et intelligi debent verba secundum illum sensum quem solent recte intelligentibus generare.*" The latter part of the Decretal Panormitanus interpreted as bearing a relation to the penitential forum, in which the marriage discussed in the Decretal was to be held as void. He forthwith added the advice: ". . . *debet tamen sacerdos in foro animae illum inducere ut consentiat de novo, et sic ut purget dolum ab eo commissum* . . ."[29]

Panormitanus clearly revealed, however, that he was not unaware of the opinion which in later centuries was to become the prevailing one. He admitted that there was another way of understanding the Decretal, namely, that the entire

---

[27]Van Hove, *op. cit.*, p. 473.

[28]*Commentaria in Quinque Libros Decretalium* (5 vols. in 7, Venetiis, 1588), Lib. IV, tit. I, cap. 26, n. 6 (hereafter cited *Commentaria).*

[29]*Loc. cit.*

Decretal bore a relation to the judicial forum, the first part of it simply stating the case, and the second part deciding it. But thereupon he listed his reasons for rejecting that interpretation. The listed reasons were substantially those which had been advanced by all the other decretalists who had resorted to the interpretation that originated with Hostiensis. If the marriage was to be declared invalid in the external forum, then its invalidity had to be substantiated by solid proof. Such proof was not sufficiently furnished through the sole confession of the guilty party, least of all when the other party had truly intended to contract a valid marriage.[80]

Finally, Panormitanus summarized what may very well be accepted as the attitude of all the decretalists on the subject:

> Aut enim fuit iusta causa protestandi; puta metus, et iuvat protestatio, nec ab ea videtur recessurum per contrarium factum . . . nisi postmodum sequatur copula . . . Aut non suberat iusta causa protestandi, et procedit determinatio glossae.''[81]

The influence of the nineteenth Ecumenical Council, although perceptible in many fields of canonical legislation, was not of great import relative to the question of fictitious consent for marriage. While the Tridentine Council clearly defined several dogmatic points with reference to marriage,[82] and introduced new norms governing the manifestation of matrimonial consent,[83] it nevertheless was silent regarding the simulation of consent. The reason for this silence apparently was the fact that there was nothing, at least regarding the substantial law, to be added to what had already been stated in the Decretal *"Tua Nos."* Indeed this Decretal remained

---

[80]*Commentaria*, Lib. IV, tit. I, cap. 26, n. 7: "Quare autem hic creditur doloso in foro iudiciali?....Sed ille intellectus mihi non placet quia ubi praesumptio est contra confitentem potest recipi confessio quatenus facit contra se....hic enim erat praesumptio contra illum confitentem, eo quod illicite extorsit copulam carnalem et quod in propria persona desponsaverit."

[81]*Ibidem*, n. 9.

[82]Sess. XXIV, *de sacramento matrimonii.*

[83]Sess. XXIV, *de ref. matrim.*, *cap.* 1.

the sole legislation on the subject until the Code of Canon Law.

The canonists of the post-Tridentine period, especially Thomas Sanchez (1550-1610),[34] contributed much to the jurisprudence of the question of total simulation, and they are still cited by the Rota in this regard.[35] Since the Code changed nothing of the substance of Innocent's decretal (indeed it could not since its doctrine reflects the natural law), the doctrine of total simulation as proposed by these writers remains of more than historical interest. For this reason their works will be referred to in the present study in the same manner as are those of the commentators on the Code of Canon Law.

---

[34]Sanchez wrote his *De Sancto Matrimonii Sacramento* about the beginning of the seventeenth century, and the work came to be considered by the Roman Curia as among the classical works on marriage. The first edition was that of 1602 at Genoa, and the last seems to have been that of 1759 at Lyons. Cf. Van Hove, *Prolegomena*, p. 557; *The Catholic Encyclopedia* (15 vols. with Index and 2 supplements, New York, 1907-1922), XIII, 427-428; J. F. von Schulte, *Die Geschichte der Quellen und Literatur des canonischen Rechts* (3 vols., Stuttgart, 1875-1880), III, 737.

[35]Cf. S. R. R., XXIII (1931), 293, n. 4; S. R. R., XVIII (1926), 254, n. 5; S. R. R., XVII (1925), 378, n. 8; S. R. R., III (1911), 14, n. 17.

CHAPTER II

THE NATURE OF TOTAL SIMULATION

The essential and constitutive element of any contract is the legitimately manifested consent of the contracting parties. As a contract, marriage is governed by the laws which concern contracts.[1] Hence a marriage cannot be effected unless a true matrimonial consent is manifested by means of words or signs.[2]

The essence of the total simulation of matrimonial consent consists in the fact that there is a discrepancy or lack of conformity between the external act by which marriage is contracted and the interior act of the will. Thus total simulation takes place when a person externally and seriously manifests signs of marital consent, but at the same time not only does not consent to the marriage, but positively intends not to marry *(intentio non contrahendi)*[3]

The concept of a simulated consent thus presupposes the fact of the celebration of the marriage, that is, that the consent was externally manifested in the manner prescribed by the law. If, instead of manifesting a will to marry at the time of the ceremony, a party disclaimed any intention

---

[1] S. R. R., XXIX (1937), 676, n. 5.

[2] St. Thomas, *Summa Theologica*, Pars III, Suppl., q. 45, art. 2.

[3] "Quod si matrimonialis consensus exterius quidem exprimitur, sed re non habetur, dicitur fieri simulatio. Quae totalis et ideo proprii nominis simulatio est. cum contrahens intentionem non habet contrahendi."—S. R. R., XXI (1929), 260, n. 3. Cf. Gasparri, *De Matrimonio*, II, 814; Coronata, *De Sacramentis* ,III n. 455; Cappello,*De Sacramentis*, III, n. 593; Wernz-Vidal, *Ius Matrimoniale*, n. 460; De Smet, *De Sponsalibus et Matrimonio*, n. 533; Heylen, *Tractatus De Matrimonio* (ed. nona, Mechliniae: H. Dessain, 1945), p. 212 (hereafter this work will be referred to as *De Matrimonio)*; Payen, *De Matrimonio*, II, n. 1667; Bayón, *Tractatus Canonico-Moralis de Sacramento Matrimonii* (2 vols in 1, ed. 1931, Madrid: Editorial del C. De Maria), I, n. 812 (hereafter cited *De Matrimonio)*; Bouscaren-Ellis, *Canon Law* (Milwaukee: The Bruce Publishing Company, 1946), p. 506.

of contracting marriage he could not be accused of simulation. However, if the denial could not be heard or seen distinctly, and at the same time other external signs of consent were offered, this would be sufficient to constitute a case of total simulation. In such an instance there would have been an apparent and serious manifestation of consent.[4]

Article I

The Intention in Total Simulation

"*At si aluterutra vel utraque pars positivo voluntatis actu excludat matrimonium ipsum . . . invalide contrahit.*"—canon 1086, §2.

The second paragraph of canon 1086 clearly implies that only a positive intention of not contracting marriage nullifies the effect of an external manifestation of consent.

A positive intention may be defined as a resolute act of the will whereby a person takes a definite stand regarding the object in question.[5] A positive intention may be an actual, a virtual, or a habitual intention. An *actual intention* is one that is elicited at the time that the act is being performed, so that it directly and immediately causes the act. If a person acts under the influence of an actual intention that was formed, not at the moment the act was performed, but at some previous time, he is said to possess a *virtual intention.* Thus a *virtual intention* is one that, though previously formed, was never recalled and remains in force at the time the act is placed, in such a manner that in the absence of this intention the act would not have been performed at all. A *habitual intention,* like a virtual intention, has its origin in an actual intention of the past. But in the case of a habitual intention, the actual intention of the past, though not recalled, has been interrupt-

---

4S. R. R., XXIX (1932), 153, n. 2.

5Griese, *The Marriage Contract and the Procreation of Offspring* (The Catholic University of America Canon Law Studies, n. 226, Washington, D.C.: The Catholic University of America Press, 1946), p. 55.

ed in such a manner that its efficacy is considered to have ceased. Consequently a habitual intention has no influece on the act being performed, and it can be had by a person who is sleeping or intoxicated, or by one who has lost the use of reason. A virtual and a habitual intention have therefore two requisites in common, namely, that an actual intention has been elicited at some time in the past, and that this actual intention has not been recalled. However the notion of a virtual intention includes a third element, to wit, that some influence of the actual intention remains and moves the faculties to the performance of the present act.[6]

Unlike the foregoing, a **negative intention** is not a true act of the will at all, since it consists in a lack of inclination on the part of the will towards a determined object. Like a habitual intention it has no influence whatsoever upon the act being performed.[7] Perhaps the most common form in which a negative intention appears, at least in relation to matrimony, is the interpretative intention. An example will illustrate this notion.

A man married a woman whom he did not love, solely because he believed that he was responsible for her pregnant condition. After the marriage he discovered that the woman had deceived him and that she was not pregnant at all. In his petition for the nullity of his marriage he stated before the Rota that the only reason for his consent was her alleged condition, and since that condition did not exist, he requested that the marriage be declared invalid.[8]

---

[6]Ferraris, *Prompta Bibliotheca Canonica Iuridica, Moralis, Theologica, necnon Ascetica Polemica Rubricistica, Historica* (9 vols., Romae, 1885-1899), V, v. *intentio;* S. R. R., IV (1912), 238, n. 6; Cappello, *De Sacramentis*, I, n. 39; Payen, *De Matrimonio*, II, n. 1675; Bouscaren-Ellis, *Canon Law*, p. 506. Griese (*op. cit.* p. 59) has interpreted this passage of Ferraris in another manner. Gasparri considers a habitual intention as the equivalent of a virtual intention (*De Matrimonio*, II, 781). Most authors however teach that it is more akin to the interpretative intention, insofar as neither of these has any influence on the act being performed.

[7]"Dicitur actu positivo voluntatis, ut excludatur actus mere negativus qui reipsa non exsistit, cum consistat in defectu tendentiae seu inclinationis ex parte voluntatis in determinatum obiectum."—Capello, *De Sacramentis*, III, n. 598. Cf. also S. R. R., XXIV (1932), 109, n. 3.

[8]S. R. R., XXVI (1934), 408-416.

"Error concerning the motive reason of a contract, that precedes or gives rise to the contract, particularly in cases of deception, is converted into what is called an interpretative *involuntarium.* This meant that if the deception had been known beforehand it most certainly would have deterred the party from contracting the marriage.'"[9] Such an interpretative intention, since it is merely negative, does not affect the validity of the consent, and thus the validity of the marriage was upheld in the case.[10]

Similarly, if a woman marries a man who fraudulently represents himself as wealthy, and even if she consents to marriage precisely because she believes him to be wealthy, the fraud does not nullify the marriage.[11] While it is quite evident that the intention of the party who is deceived into marrying would not nullify the contract unless a condition had been placed to forestall such a fraud, the intention of the deceiver, on the other hand, may be more difficult to determine. This is illustrated by a case which was decided by the Rota in 1925 and, on appeal, in 1927, and again in 1928.[12]

A certain marriage had been contracted invalidly, but the invalidity remained unknown to both parties. During the first World War the man served with the military forces, and subsequently the rumour was circulated that he had been killed in battle. However, there was evidence that this rumour originated with the man's wife, who could not offer satisfactory proof that the source of her knowledge had been reliable. In short, there was some doubt whether she believed that her

9Doheny, *Canonical Procedure in Matrimonial Cases* (2 vols., Vol. I, *Formal Procedure*, Vol. II, *Informal Procedure*, Milwaukee: Bruce, 1938, 1944), I, 550 (hereafter cited *Canonical Procedure)*.

10S. R. R., XXVI (1934), 415-6, n. 14.

11Andrew Quinn, "Defects in Marriage Consent"—*The Jurist*, Washington, D.C.: The Catholic University of America, 1941—), V (1945), 550.

12S. R. R., XVII (1925), 293-295; S. R. R., XIX (1927), 192-198; S. R. R., XX (1928), 106-112. The earliest of these decisions declared the nullity, but the latter two upheld the validity of the marriage. The case is listed under *error* in the index of Volume XX of the Rota Decisions. Cf. Bouscaren, *The Canon Law Digest* (2 vols., Milwaukee: Bruce, 1934-1943), II, 301; Doheny, *Canonical Procedure*, I, 562-564.

husband was dead. After she had contracted marriage with another man, her first husband reappeared. The remarks regarding the woman's intention, which are contained in one of these decisions, are pertinent to the present question. The Rota claimed that, even with the supposition that the woman knew that her former husband was alive, and that she had spread false rumours of his death, nevertheless it cannot be concluded that she simulated marital consent with the second man. In spite of her error regarding her freedom to marry, she could still have elicited a true consent to marriage. To prove simulation one must prove the existence of a positive will that excludes marriage. The fraud inflicted on the second man does not necessarily indicate that the woman simulated matrimonial consent.[13]

It is apparent that only an actual or virtual intention has any influence on the act being performed. Consequently, in so far as matrimonial consent is concerned, a habitual intention and a negative intention are to be disregarded.[14]

The notion of total simulation implies that the apparent manifestation of consent is a deliberate human act, which can be effected only by means of a positive intention. The reason for the falsity of the apparent manifestation is the fact that it does not correspond to the simulator's knowledge of the concomitant existence of his intention of not marrying. As stated, the intention of not marrying must also be a positive intention. Therefore total simulation implies the existence of two distinct acts of the will, namely, the positive intention of not marrying, and the positive intention of giving an apparent manifestation of consent, which manifestation the simulator knows to be false. One cannot conceive of a case of total simulation in which the simulator did not have the intention of simulating. The act of simulation must at the same time connote the presence of a lie. Simulation never consists of an inactivity in which the will remains merely passive,

[13]S. R. R., XX (1928), 110, n. 6.
[14]S. R. R., XVIII (1926), 230, n. 2; S. R. R., XVI (1924), 59, n. 2.

and thus such a concept as that of a purely material simulation cannot exist.[15]

Since a positive act of the will is required for total simulation, it is immediately apparent that such an act can not remain unknown to the agent. A person guilty of total simulation is naturally aware of the simulation, at least at the time the act was placed, just as he is aware of any of his deliberate acts at the time of their performance. The claim that one was not conscious of any simulation indicates that total simulation was absent.[16]

There is, however, one instance in which this usual adjunct of total simulation may not be present. It is the case wherein a person married under the influence of grave fear. A person who was forced to submit to the ceremony may have been so emotionally perturbed at the time, that after the wedding he is unable to declare whether he actually did or

---

[15]"......simulatio consistere nequit in intertia voluntatis passive se habentis, sed actum e contra et exercitium voluntatis vere supponit dictante ad rem can. 1086 § 2: 'Si alterutra vel utraque pars positivo voluntatis actu excludat matrimonium ipsum, aut omne ius ad coniugalem actum, vel essentialem aliquam matrimonii proprietatem, invalide contrahit.' Quare ad simulationis essentiam, in iuris conceptu, proprie pertinet quod in agente discrepantia seu difformitas verificetur inter actum exteriorem, quo matrimonium contrahitur, et consensum interiorem, quatenus interior consensus, per actum voluntatis elicitus, vim detrahit actui, qui externe ponitur. Hinc simulatio pure materialis, obiective nempe et materialiter inspecta, de qua loquuntur patroni, haud admittitur, cum concipi nequeat simulatio absque simulandi intentione, seu absque mendacio; per simulationem siquidem contrahens verbis aliud quam mente profitetur."—S. R. R., XXIII (1931), 196, n. 6. Cf. also S. R. R., XXIX (1937), 315, n. 2; S.R.R., XXIII (1931), 293-304. A falsehood would not be imputed to the simulator in the case of a jocose consent that *per accidens* was not perceived as such or in the case wherein the simulation was morally justifiable (e.g., because of the influence of grave fear).

[16]"Quare praetensa simulatio latuisset ipsum simulantem; quod tamen admitti nequit. Aliquis potest quidem ignorare vim irritantem, quae coniuncta est cum impedimentis matrimonii vel cum exclusione unius alteriusve ex bonis essentialibus matrimonii, sed fictio totalis matrimonii non potest non cognosci ab ipso auctore simulationis. Etenim haec simulatio exigit in contrahente positivum voluntatis actum oppositum verbis in celebratione matrimonii adhibitis et consensum per se manifestantibus, qui eliminat et destruit intrinsecam efficientiam consensus externe positi ; palam vero est tantum facinus auctorem non potuisse latere. Sin auem contrahens simulationis sibi conscius non fit hoc indicat veram simulationem abesse"—S.R.R., XXVIII (1936) 111, n. 13.

did not consent to marriage. Such a state of mental confusion would perhaps be more apt to occur among less intelligent persons. [17]

The two elements which comprise total simulation are the following: an apparently serious manifestation of consent by means of words or signs, and a positive internal act of the will that excludes what is expressed.[18] It is evident that a fictitious or simulated consent is incapable of effecting a valid marriage, since without a true consent the matrimonial contract cannot exist. This is a principle of the natural law, and thus applies also to the marriages of non-Christians.[19]

In contrast to the simplicity of the concept of total simulation, the proof of the fact that a marital consent was fictitious usually presents many difficulties in a particular case.[20] In evaluating the evidence for and against the existence of an internal intention, it is not impossible that some other defect of consent could be confused with total simulation. For this reason it may be of advantage to compare total simulation with some of the other forms of deficient consent, which may constitute distinct grounds for impugning the validity of marriage.

---

[17] "Contingere autem potest ut qui metu gravi commotus fuerit, praesertim si rudis ingenii sit, non valeat declarare utrum consensum simulaverit, an consensum re vera praestiterit, quamquam ex metu elicitum"—S. R. R., XVII (1925), 68, n. 2. Cf. also S. R. R., XVI (1924), 383, n. 2; S. R. R., XIX (1927), 316, n. 3.

[18] S. R. R., XVII (1925), 175, n. 3.

[19] "Patet igitur iam ex natura rei consensum fictum seu simulatum nihil efficere, quoniam quod obiective non existit, sed tantum fingitur, incapax est ad constituendum coniugium."—S. R. R., XXIII (1931), 225, n. 3. Cf. also S. R. R., XXIX (1937), 150, n. 4; S. R. R., XXVI (1934), 452, nn. 4-5; Sanchez, *De Matrimonio*, Lib. II, Disp. XXV, n. 3; Schmalzgrueber, *Ius Ecclesiasticum Universum*, Lib. IV, Tit. I, n. 264; Laymann, *Theologia Moralis* (6 ed., 2 vols., Bambergae, 1669), Lib. V, Tract. X, Par. II, Cap. VI, n. 1; Gonzalez-Gellez, *Commentaria Perpetua in Singulis Textus Quinque Librorum Decretalium Gregorii IX* (5 vols. in 4, Vol. IV, Venetiis, 1699), Lib. IV, Tit. I, Cap. 26 (hereafter cited *Commentaria*).

[20] "At simulatio, cum sit factum internum, externae et liberae expressioni contrarium, difficillime in iudicio probatur"— S. R. R., XXIX (1937), 150, n. 4; cf. also S. R. R., XIX (1927), 215, n. 2: "........tota quaestio versatur in probatione huius simulationis."

Article II

Total Simulation and Other Defects of Consent Compared

Since *defective consent* (*defectus consensus*) is a general term which embraces any *vitium consensus,* it does not seem practicable to impugn a marriage simply on this ground without any further specification.[21] This general term embraces the following specific invalidating elements: absence of consent or insufficient consent, total and partial simulation, unfulfilled condition, force and fear, ignorance and error. Simulation of consent is therefore a species of deficient consent.[22] Since ignorance and error can vitiate consent only because of a lack of due knowledge on the part of the intellect, they do not pertain to the present subject, and thus will not be considered in the following comparison.

A defect of consent may be positive or negative. If it is positive, the will positively excludes consent, and this is called simulation. If it is negative, it is so precisely because the will abstains from consenting.[23] With regard to unfulfilled condition and force and fear, although it is true that there is an act of the will in these cases, nevertheless the invalidity is due to some extrinsic influence. At this point it is the lack of an intention to contract marriage, considered in itself, that is at issue. This negative defect of consent whereby the will abstains from acting, may be called the absence of consent. When there is no internal act of consent inasmuch as the will is neutral, it follows that there is also no external manifestation of consent.[24] If there is an external act at all, it is not a fully deliberate human act.

---

[21]Roberti, "Quaestiones quaedam de identificatione actionum ob vitia consensus in causa matrimonialibus"—*Apollinaris* (Romae, 1928—), VI (1933), 106.

[22]Gasparri, *De Matrimonio*, nn. 782, ff.; Heylen, *De Matrimonio*, pp. 192-4; Coronata, *De Sacramentis*, III, n. 430; Cappello, *De Sacramentis*, III, nn. 575-6; Payen, *De Matrimonio*, II, nn. 1597-1603; De Smet, *De Sponsalibus et Matrimonio*, nn. 100-102; Bayón, *De Matrimonio*, I. nn. 753-761; Doheny, *Canonical Procedure*, I, 550; S. R. R., XXIII (1931), 195, n. 3.

[23]S. R. R., XXVI (1934), 4, n. 3; S. R. R., XXII (1930), 155, n. 2.

[24]S. R. R., XXIX (1937), 734-5, n. 2-3; S. R. R., XXVII (1935), 78-9, n. 5; S. R. R., XXVI (1934), 81, n. 3.

For the validity of marriage there must be a legitimate manifestation of consent. That it be manifested in words is merely for licitness, as is the obligation of following the Ritual. Any type of manifestation suffices for validity.[25] It may have happened that one of the parties has remained mute, or has uttered unintelligible sounds at the moment prescribed for the manifestation of consent. In such a case the attendant circumstances may reveal whether this conduct was due to timidity or self-consciousness, in which eventuality the manifestation may have been supplied by means of positive signs other than words, or whether it occurred as a result of the fact that the person did not actually give his consent to the marriage. In either case there is no question of fictitious consent: mere silence is not to be confused with simulated consent. In a case of the absence of consent, the will is neutral, whereas the positive intention of not contracting is necessary to constitute a case of total simulation.[26] The simulator, in speaking contrary to his true intention, contradicts himself in so far as he externally and fictitiously manifests a consent which he does not internally will. The one who remains silent, since he manifests nothing, does not contradict himself, and unless his consent is manifested in some other way, he is not considered to have consented to marriage.[27] In the case of the absence of consent, a party is considered to have acted as an automaton if he placed any external act that may have been interpreted as a manifestation of consent.[28]

If the external manifestation of consent is a fully deliberate act it must be the effect of one of two positive intentions, namely, the positive intention to simulate, or the intention to manifest a true consent. It is sometimes claimed that a party did not fully consent to marriage, but that he only partly consented, because he was greatly perturbed at

[25] De Smet, *De Sponsalibus et Matrimonio*, n. 103.

[26] S. R. R., XXVII (1935), 624, n. 9.

[27] S. R. R., XXVI (1934), 81, n. 3; Chelodi, *Ius Canonicum de Matrimonio* (5 ed. recognita et aucta a Pio Ciprotti, Vincenza: Società Anonima Tipografica Editrice, 1947), n. 121.

[28] Cf. S. R. R., XXVII (1935), 625, n. 13.

the time of the ceremony. Such a partial consent, in so far as it signifies at least some intention of marrying, is certainly not the equivalent of a positive intention of not marrying, and hence cannot provide the basis for a case of total simulation. If the consent was not sufficient for the contracting of marriage, then it seems that the manifestation of consent was also somewhat indeliberate. The only count upon which such a marriage could be impugned seems to be that of insufficient consent.

A simulated consent differs also from one that is manifested in a joking manner. The latter is had when it is apparent to the witnesses that the party (parties) had no serious intention of consenting to the marriage contract.[29] In the case of total simulation there is a serious manifestation of consent which is capable of deceiving the witnesses and the other consort. A joke, on the other hand, is either evidently a joke, or else it does not possess the nature of a joke. If it is evidently a joke, there is lacking even a true external manifestation of consent.[30] The jocose nature of the affair is usually evident from the words employed, from the manner of speaking, or from the circumstances. This may remain unperceived by the other party, but still be evident to the witnesses.[31] If it is not evidently a joke, then it is a case of total simulation, even though it may not be intended as such by the party himself.[32]

The notion of the total simulation of matrimonial consent is accurately described in the words of the terminology employed. It pertains to the subject of the consent, and consists in the fact that the external manifestation does not correspond to the internal will. Partial simulation is not necessarily related to total simulation as the part to the whole. Partial simulation derives its name, not from the subject, but from the object, of the consent. It exists when a party's marital

29 Gasparri, *De Matrimonio*, II, nn. 830-831; Cappello, *De Sacramentis*, III, n. 604; Bayón, *De Matrimonio*, I, n. 812.

30 Payen, *De Matrimonio*, II, n. 1667.

31 Wernz-Vidal, *Ius Matrimoniale*, n. 460.

32 Payen, *loc. cit.* For an example of a case of jocose consent, cf. S. C. C., *Ausculana Matrimonii*, 14. dec. 1889—*Thesaurus* CXLVIII, 865-887.

consent is directed towards something that does not possess at the same time both the essence and the essential qualities of marriage. Consequently a person would not be estopped from impugning his marriage on the ground of partial simulation simply because it had been impugned previously on the ground of total simulation, and on that score had been upheld as valid. The two forms of simulation constitute entirely distinct grounds for nullity.[33]

The purpose and the nature of many contracts are determined by the wills of the contracting parties, but this is not true of the contract of marriage.[34] The purpose and the nature of matrimony, and in consequence its essential qualities, also have been determined by Almighty God. Since the nature of marriage is not determined by the wills of the contracting parties, matrimonial consent depends on these same human wills only for its existence, and not also for its essence. The essence of matrimonial consent is defined in canon 1081. § 2: *Consensus matrimonialis est actus voluntatis quo utraque pars tradit et acceptat ius in corpus, perpetuum et exclusivum, in ordine ad actus per se aptos ad prolis generationem.* The words *ius in corpus* express the primary object of the consent, and the adjectives *perpetuum* and *exclusivum* the essential properties of matrimony.[35]

For the validity of any contract it is necessary that the consent of the contracting parties be at least implicitly directed towards the substantial object of the contract, that

---

[33]Roberti, "Quaestiones quaedam de identificatione actionum ob vitia consensus in causis matrimonialibus,"—*Apollinaris*, VI (1933), 106, n. 2.

[34]Leclercq suggests the term *contract of adherence* as applicable to those contracts which are public law institutions, the constitutions of which the parties have no power to modify. Cf. Jacques Leclercq, *Marriage and the Family* (translated by Thomas R. Hanley, 2 ed. New York and Cincinnati: Pustet, 1945), p. 31; Heinrich A. Rommen, *The Natural Law* (translated by Thomas R. Hanley, St. Louis: Herder, 1947), p. 239.

[35]Canon 1013, § 2: Essentiales matrimonii proprietates sunt unitas ac indissolubilitas, quae in matrimonio christiano peculiarem obtinent firmitatem ratione sacramenti." "Duo hi canones (1081 et 1086) arcte connectuntur. Attento enim quod matrimonium uno partium seu coniugum consensu constituatur (can. 1081, § 1), iam per se patet eum invalide contrahere qui in matrimonium consentiat aliter ac eius natura exigit."—S. R. R., XXII (1930), 670, n. 3.

is, towards everything that pertains to its essence.[36] No human power can effect a change in the nature of matrimony, and thus no one can contract a true marriage unless his act of the will in contracting embraces the complete essence of marriage.[37]

The second paragraph of canon 1081 expresses the teaching of the Church with regard to the essential elements of matrimonial consent. In their designation of these essentials, theologians and canonists have consistently adhered to the terminology first employed by Saint Augustine (354-430).[38] The phrase, *acts suitable by their very nature for the procreation of offspring,* as occurring in canon 1081, § 2, and likewise the phrase, *acts proper to conjugal life,* as employed in canon 1111, indicate the Augustinian blessing of offspring (*bonum prolis*). The references to the essential properties of marriage (canon 1013, § 2) and to the perpetuity and exclusiveness of the marital right (canon 1081, § 2) indicate the blessing of sacramental stability *(bonum sacramenti)* and the blessing of fidelity (*bonum fidei*).[39]

All three of these blessings of marriage pertain to the essence of matrimony, but not all do so in the same manner. The realization or enjoyment of the blessing of sacramental stability (i.e., the essential quality of indissolubility) is had from the moment that the two contracting parties have exchanged a matrimonial consent. This is so because marriage cannot exist except as a stable and perpetual union. Thus indissolubility always pertains to the essence of marriage. On the contrary, the enjoyment of the other two blessings *(bonum*

---

[36]Benedictus XIV, *De Synodo Dioecesana* (2 vols., Romae, 1806), Lib. XIII, cap. 22, n. 7.

[37]"Homo enim naturam ipsam matrimonii a Deo statutam immutare nequit, neque istud sacrum foedus inire potest, nisi in contrahendo eius actus voluntatis amplectatur totam essentiam matrimonii."—S. R. R., XXIV (1932), 159, n. 3.

[38]Cf. *De Bono Conjugali*, Lib. Unicus, cap. 3—*CSEL*, XLI, 190; *De Genesi ad Litteram*, Lib. IX, cap. 7,—*CSEL*, XXVIII, pars prima, 275-6; *De Peccato Originali contra Pelagium*, Lib. II, cap. 34,—*MPL*, XLIV, 404; *De Nuptiis et Concupiscentia*, Lib. I, cap. XVII,—CSEL, XLII, 231; *De Bono Conjugali*, Lib. Unicus, cap. 18—*CSEL*, XLI, 214-215.

[39]Griese, *The Marriage Contract and the Procreation of Offspring*, p. 6.

prolis et bonum fidei) does not pertain to the essence of matrimony, since the realization of these depends upon the use of the marriage right, which in turn does not directly pertain to the substance of the contract.[40] Hence, regarding the blessings of offspring and fidelity, there is a real distinction between the existence of these obligations and their fulfillment.[41]

For the validity of a marriage only the acceptance of the obligations is necessary. Each contracting party must grant to the other the right to his or her body for the performance of the act which by nature is directed to the procreation of offspring. Under pain of invalidity this right must be granted exclusively and until death. As long as this is done, the intention to abuse marriage, by contraception or adultery, for example, simply amounts to an intention of not fulfilling the obligations promoting the blessings of offspring or of fidelity respectively. This latter intention, though gravely sinful, does not nulify marital consent.[42]

As a consequence of this Thomistic distinction, it is immediately evident that in this matter there are two possible intentions that may be had by a party in contracting marriage. One may indeed intend to contract marriage, but at the same time have a positive intention of not assuming the obligations essential to marriage. On the other hand, one may intend both to contract marriage and to assume the essential obligations thereof, but also intend not to fulfill these obligations,

---

[40] St. Thomas, *Summa Theologica*, Pars III, Suppl., q. 49, art. 3; Sanchez, *De Matrimonio*, Lib. II, Disp. XXIX, n. 12.

[41] Cf. S. R. R., XVII (1925), 374, n. 2.

[42] A decision of the Rota given in the year 1932 corrects some false notions concerning the blessings of offspring and fidelity that had been proposed by the Defender of the Bond of the lower tribunal. The fact that a person has the intention of rendering the right to a *copula perfecta* does not preclude the possibility that he has an *intentio contra bonum prolis*. If one party had the intention of preventing the generation of children in any way, and at the time of the contract yielded the marital right with this reservation, the marriage would be invalid. It was also pointed out that an intention contrary to the blessing of fidelity is constituted not only through a reservation of the right to contract more than one bond of marriage, but also through a reservation of the right to have carnal relations with others.—S. R. R., XXIV (1932), 67, n. 5.

or, in other words, the intention is that of abusing the marriage.

Partial simulation of matrimonial consent is had when a person externally manifests consent to marriage and internally wills to marry, but positively intends not to bind himself to one or other of the obligations essential to marriage. This is the *intentio non sese obligandi.* Distinct from this is the case wherein a person gives an external consent to marriage, actually intending to bind himself to the marital obligations, but intending to be unfaithful to those obligations, or not to fulfill them *(intentio non implendi).* These two, namely, the *intentio non sese obligandi* and the *intentio non implendi,* together with the *intentio non contrahendi,* comprise the three possible forms under which simulation may appear.[43] The intention of not contracting is simulation in the most strict sense: it is called *total simulation,* and it possesses, of course, an invalidating effect. The latter two are referred to as *partial simulation,* or simulation in a wider or less proper sense..[44]

The mere intention of not fulfilling the obligations assumed is not a true simulation, according to Coronata, who calls it a *simulatio improprie dicta.*[45] The reason for this terminology is the fact that the intention of not fulfilling the marital obligations assumed does not in any way invalidate the matrimonial contract. In this basic effect it is unlike the intention of not contracting marriage, and also unlike the intention of not assuming the marital obligations, both of which inevitably result in the nullity of the marriage.[46]

---

[43]Gasparri, *De Matrimonio,* II, nn. 825-827; Cappello, *De Sacramentis,* III, n. 598; Payen, *De Matrimonio,* II, nn. 1674-1676; Wernz-Vidal, *Ius Matrimoniale,* n. 461; De Smet, *De Sponsalibus et Matrimonio,* nn. 155-6, 534; Heylen, *De Matrimonio,* p. 214; Bayón, *De Matrimonio,* I, nn. 819-821; Coronata, *De Sacramentis,* III, nn. 458-9; Bouscaren-Ellis, *Canon Law,* p. 506; Vermeersch-Creusen, *Epitome Iuris Canonici* (3 vols., 5 ed., Mechliniae: H. Dessain, 1933-1936), II, n. 374; Ayrinhac and Lydon, *Marriage Legislation in the New Code of Canon Law* (ed. 1932, New York: Benziger Brothers), n. 204; Chelodi, *De Matrimonio,* nn. 116-117.

[44]Cf. S. R. R., XXI (1929), 145, n. 4; S. R. R., XXIX (1937), 560, nn. 2-6; S. R. R., XXVI (1934), 466, n. 2.

[45]*Loc. cit.*

[46]Cf. S. R. R., XXVI (1934), 452, nn. 4-5; S. R. R., XIX (1927), 172, n. 4; S. R. R., XVII (1925), 220, n. 5.

The distinguishing characteristic of both total and partial simulation is the contradiction that exists between what is internally willed and what is externally manifested. What has been said in reference to total simulation regarding the necessity of a positive intention if there is to be a nullifying effect is equally applicable to partial simulation.[47] When a party has the positive intention of contracting marriage, he is presumed to also have the intention of contracting marriage with its essential qualities. If the marriage is to be declared null on the ground of partial simulation, it must be proved that one of the parties positively intended to exclude at least one of the essential obligations of marriage.[48]

Simple error regarding the essential obligations is not to be confused with simulation; such error has no effect on the validity of the consent.[49] Likewise a habitual intention or disposition, though it be contrary to one or all of the essential obligations, does not suffice to nullify the intention of contracting.[50]

Both total and partial simulation invalidate matrimonial consent, but the reasons for the nullity are not identical in the two instances. In the case of total simulation the simulator positively intends to present only a fictitious manifestation of consent, and the contract is void because a true consent is entirely absent. In a partial simulation of consent the simulator has indeed the general intention of contracting marriage, but this intent is nullified through a second positive intention which

---

[47] Cf. S. R. R., XXII (1930), 353, n. 7; *ibidem*, 375, n. 6; Gasparri, *De Matrimonio*, II, n. 825.

[48] "Ad matrimonii valorem non exigitur quod contrahens expresse, seu positivo voluntatis actu, coniugii proprietates acceptet, cum haec omnia accepta subintelligantur ex ipso facto celebrationis contractus; necesse tamen est, quod nihil in consensu ponat, quod iisdem qualitatibus essentialibus adversetur seu quod nullam ex iis positivo voluntatis actu excludat."—S. R. R., XXIII (1931), 482, n. 2. Cf. also, S. R. R. XXVI (1934), 674, n. 5; S. R. R., XXII (1930), 373-4, n. 3; S. R. R., XX (1928), 393, n. 2; S. R. R., XVII (1925), 220, n. 5.

[49] Canon 1084: "Simplex error circa matrimonii unitatem vel indissolubilitatem aut sacramentalem dignitatem, etsi det causam contractui, non vitiat consensum matrimonialem."

[50] S. R. R., XXIII (1931), 300, n. 19; Bouscaren-Ellis, *Canon Law*, p. 506.

is more specific, namely, the intention which is contrary to one of the essential obligations.[51]

Although the two types both bear the name of simulation, and although both are causes of invalidity in the marriage contract, they nevertheless are two basically distinct concepts. Total simulation is nothing else than that which the word implies, a fictitious manifestation of consent. It pertains to the subject of the consent, that is, to the person who elicits the act, inasmuch as his external behavior is directly contradictory to his internal intention. The simulation which is called partial refers rather to the object of the consent, in so far as what is consented to does not comprise the essential totality towards which the consent must be directed in order that marriage be validly contracted. Since they are essentially distinct, the two forms of simulation constitute separate grounds for impugning the validity of a marriage. Moreover, partial simulation may provide the basis for three distinct *actiones* corresponding to the three essential blessings of marriage. This follows from the fact that there may be as many judicial actions introduced as there are juridical facts which could effect the nullity of a particular marriage.

Another aspect under which the two types of simulation differ is in reference to the simulator's knowledge of the invalidity of the marriage. It has been seen that with one exception[52] it is impossible for one who has totally simulated matrimonial consent to be unaware of the consequent nullity of his marriage. This is not true of partial simulation. A person who positively excludes one of the essential obligations of marriage will certainly be aware of that exclusion, but he may not realize that the excluded obligation is essential to a valid marriage.[53] It will be noted that here it is not a question merely

51Gasparri, *De Matrimonio*, II, n. 825; Cappello, *De Sacramentis*, III, n. 598; Coronata, *De Sacramentis*, III, n. 458; Heylen, *De Matrimonio*, p. 214; Wernz-Vidal, *Ius Matrimoniale*, n. 461; Payen, *De Matrimonio*, II, n. 1675; B. Pellegrini, "De Intentione Bono Sacramenti Adversa Ejusdemque Probatione in Iudicio ad Normam Can. 1086"—*Jus Pontificium* (Romae, 1921-1940), IX (1929), 306-311.

52The possible exception is the case wherein the party has been influenced by grave fear.

53S. R. R., XXVIII (1936), 111, n. 14.

of ignorance regarding an essential quality of marriage, for such ignorance has no invalidating effect on the consent.

Notwithstanding these differences, the distinction between total and partial simulation remains merely theoretical in many cases. In practice, indeed, it frequently happens that a person who has apparently committed a partial simulation is guilty of a total simulation in reality. The following is an actual case decided by the Rota.[54]

A certain woman had been intimate with a married man who was awaiting a decree of civil divorce from his wife. The woman's parents were unwilling to consent to her marriage with this man, and she had not attained the age prescribed for legal emancipation. When it was suggested that she marry another man (the plaintiff in the present case), she externally acquiesced in order to be free of the authority of her parents. In contracting this marriage the woman excluded entirely the obligation of conjugal fidelity, since she intended to continue relations with her lover. At the same time she intended to procure a civil divorce in order to contract a civil marriage with the same lover after his marriage had been civilly dissolved. Theoretically she committed only a double act of partial simulation, but in fact she was considered as having totally simulated her matrimonial consent, and it was on this ground that the marriage was declared invalid.[55]

Those cases of partial simulation in which the simulator excludes all three essential obligations seem to be tantamount to a total simulation. Rarely, if ever, would it happen that a person would exclude both the essence and the essential qualities of marriage and still intend to contract marriage. Hence the Rota considers these cases as instances of total simulation.[56]

---

[54] S. R. R., XXVII (1935), 519-530.

[55] *Ibidem*, p. 521, n. 3; 530, n. 18.

[56] Cf. S. R. R., XXIX (1937), 557-560, nn. 2-6; S. R. R., XXVI (1934), 466,n. 2; S. R. R., XXIII (1931), 85, n. 19; S. R. R., VII (1915), 203, n. 10. In another case, positive intentions contrary to the blessings of offspring and sacramental stability were proven to have existed, as well as the fact of adultery after marriage, yet no positive intention against

The intention to contract a marriage that is to endure only for a determined period of time is directly contrary to the essential quality of indissolubility, and hence is a type of partial simulation. However, if the period of time is extremely brief, for example, if a party intends the marriage to bind for only a few days, this intention is the equivalent of total simulation. In such cases, regardless of whether the simulation is committed for the satisfaction of lustful desires or for any other reason, it is far more probable that the party intends not to marry, rather than that he intends merely to contract a dissoluble union.[57]

Total simulation, with which the present study deals, is also distinct from conditional consent. The former is no consent at all, but only an apparent consent. In simulation there is an act of the will which is psychologically complete, but because it is the antithesis of matrimonial consent it does not produce a valid marriage. Conditional consent, on the other hand, is a true consent, though it is not a pure consent, in so far as the production of its effect, i.e., matrimony, depends on the fulfillment of the condition placed.[58]

It is evident that the exclusion of one of the essential obligations of marriage need not be in the form of a condition in order to have an invalidating effect. For this it is sufficient that there be an explicit contrary act of the will, though

---

the blessing of fidelity was shown to have existed at the time of the wedding. The Decision refers simply to simulation.—S. R. R., XXIII (1931), 286-292. Another case of the same year presents an instance in which evidence which disproved the existence of an *intentio non contrahendi* was also considered as establishing the fact that an intention contrary to the blessings of offspring and sacramental stability was also absent.—S. R. R., XXIII (1931), 292-304.

[57]S. R. R., XXVI (1934), 73, n. 6. Cf. also S. R. R., XXII (1930), 386, n. 3: "Exclusa igitur indissolubilitate, simulatio foret partialis; verum consensus ita limitatus, in animo viri qui utique sciebat matrimonium esse indissolubile, recidere videtur in casum simulationis totalis."

[58]Gasparri, *De Matrimonio*. II, n. 878; Wernz-Vidal, *Ius Matrimoniale* nn. 510 ff.; Cappello, *De Sacramentis*, III, nn. 625 ff.; Coronata, *De Sacramentis*, III, n. 457; Payen, *De Matrimonio*, II, n. 1725; Timlin, *Conditional Matrimonial Consent*, The Catholic University of America Canon Law Studies, n. 89 (Washington, D.C.: Catholic University of America, 1934), *passim*.

the existence of a contrary condition is more easily proved than that of a positive intention.[59] A person who subjects his consent to a condition which is contrary to an essential property of matrimony may obviously remain unaware of the consequent nullity of his marriage. Under this aspect conditional consent is like partial, but unlike total, simulation.

It may be difficult in certain particular cases to determine whether a marriage is null because of fictitious consent or whether its invalidity is due to the influence of force and fear.[60]

It is admitted by all that physical force or fear which eliminates the use of reason invalidates marriage by the law of nature.[61] These cases could rarely be confused with total simulation, since a legitimate manifestation of consent is lacking in them. The present consideration is confined to the more common case of a moral force, which does not remove the use of reason. As has been seen, in the case of total simulation the contract is void by the natural law because of the lack of the essential element of true consent. In a case of force and fear, on the contrary, there is a true consent for the one who suffers the fear positively wills to contract marriage *(coacta voluntas est semper voluntas.)*[62] The person chooses marriage rather than something else, and hence the action is voluntary *simpliciter,* but involuntary *secundum quid.* Ordinarily acts which are performed because of grave fear which is inflicted unjustly upon the person acting can be rescinded through a *restitutio in integrum.*[63] However, when it is a question of the status of persons this general norm is inapplicable,[64] and thus for the preservation of

---

[59]"Si prava voluntas inserta est in contractu per conditionem vel per pactum, facilius praestatur probatio; difficilius vero, si alter, altero nescio, suum consensum vitiavit"—S. R. R., XXV (1933), 283, n. 2. Cf. also S. R. R., XXIV (1932), 12, n. 2.

[60]Cf. S. R. R., XXV (1933), 243, n. 2; S. R. R., XVII (1925), 67-73, *passim.*

[61]Cf. Coronata, *De Sacramentis,* III, n. 480.

[62]S. R. R., XVI (1924), 68, n. 2; Gasparri, De Matrimonio, 833 ff.

[63]Canon 103, § 2.

[64]Canons 1905; 1903.

equity such actions are declared invalid *ipso iure*.[65] Wherefore, the basis of the invalidating effect of canon 1087 is not the fact that consent is entirely absent, but rather the fact that grave injury is sustained by a person's right.[66] This is certainly true if the invalidating effect is due to positive legislation alone. Moreover, even if it is held that the nullity in these cases is a dictate of the natural law, it must be admitted that, though insufficient, there is at least some consent for the marriage.

In consequence of the objective difference between a marriage that is null because of total simulation and one that is invalid by reason of force and fear, it is evident that the two cannot coexist in a particular case.[67]

One who enters marriage because of fear generally elicits a true consent, though it be imperfectly voluntary and inefficacious to effect the sacred bond. (It is presumed that the conditions of canon 1087 are fulfilled). However it sometimes happens that the party who is influenced by the grave fear is so opposed to the marriage extorted by it that he either places no consent at all or simulates the consent.[68] Therefore grave fear is to be reckoned among the potential causes of simulation. In certain instances it may be impossible to determine whether the person suffering the fear actually did or did not consent to the marriage, and thus it would be uncertain which factor actually caused the invalidity. In such cases, as long as the conditions of canon 1087 are proved to have existed, the invalidity of the marriage may be declared in spite of the doubt regarding the actual consent. This point

---

65 It is disputed whether this is a principle of the natural law, or whether it proceeds solely from positive legislation. For an analysis of the two opinions cf. Coronata, *De Sacramentis*, III, n. 480; Sangmeister, *Force and Fear as Precluding Matrimonial consent*, The Catholic University of America Canon Law Studies, n. 80 (Washington, D.C.: Catholic University of America, 1932), p. 154-163.

66 S. R. R., XVII (1925), 175, n 4.

67 "Simulatio et metus duas constituunt causas petendi, non solum inter se diversas sed et tales, quae simul stare non possint. Etenim per simulationem nullus consensus haberetur, seu consensus matrimonialis deest; per metum contra consensus quidem habetur, etsi vitiatus"—S. R. R., XXX (1938), 648, n. 3. Cf. also S. R. R., XXIV (1932), 208, n. 2.

68 S. R. R., XXVI (1934), 81, n. 3.

will be further discussed in the chapter which treats of the cause of simulation.

A marital consent which is involuntary *secundum quid* does not of itself render a marriage null. In order that this effect follow, the influence of force and fear must also be present.[69] Consequently a person who enters marriage without love, and solely to gain some advantage by so doing, cannot be said to simulate consent, unless at the same time he has the positive intention of simulating. For a valid contract it is not necessary that the parties love each other and happily enter the marriage. It is sufficient that they internally consent and manifest their consent externally in a legitimate manner.[70] A lack of love and even a positive aversion towards the other party can coexist with the deliberate intention of contracting a valid marriage.[71] A person who merely pretends to love the other party may act deceitfully and commit a form of fraud, but the validity of the marriage is not thereby affected. Fictitious love is not the equivalent of fictitious consent.[72]

In the light of the essential distinctions that have been indicated above, it is apparent that a marriage cannot be invalid on the ground of total simulation and at the same time null because of the exclusion of an essential marital obligation, or because of the absence of consent, or because of insufficient consent, or because of force and fear.[73] A person would contradict himself were he to claim that he intended

[69]S. R. R., IV (1912), 466, n. 19: "Consensus vero involuntarius tantum secundum quid non reddit matrimonium nullum, uti diximus, nisi forte intercedat impedimentum vis et metus,......"

[70]"At simulare matrimonium dici nequit ille, qui absque amore et ob solam causam utilitatis vel necessitatis aegre et invitus nuptias iniit, nisi simul positive habeat intentionem consensum simulandi. Siquidem ad valide contrahendum non requiritur, ut nupturiens alteram partem amet et libenter matrimonium ineat, sed sufficit ut interne in matrimonium consentiat et externe suum consensum rite exprimat."—S. R. R., XXIX (1937), 315, n. 2. Cf. also S. R. R., XXVII (1935), 342, n. 19; S. R. R., XXVII (1935), 622, n. 3.

[71]"At defectus amoris, et aversio positiva componi possunt cum deliberato animo matrimonium valide contrahendi."— S. R. R., IV (1912), 468, n. 22. Cf. also S. R. R., XXIX (1937), 315, n. 2.

[72]S. R. R., XXVIII (1936), 102, n. 3; 112, n. 14.

[73]Cf. S. R. R., XXVII (1935), 624, n. 9.

positively not to contract the marriage and that simultaneously he had a positive intention of excluding an essential quality, for example, that of indissolubility.[74]

Similarly, since the will is merely passive in a case of the absence of consent, this intention cannot coexist along with a total simulation, for the latter presupposes a positive act of the will.[75] Finally, that a marriage be invalid both because of force and fear and also because of total simulation is likewise an impossibility, since in the former case there is a positive will to contract a marriage.[76]. Nothwithstanding these evident differences, the Rota Decisions record instances in which certain lower tribunals declared particular marriages invalid on grounds which are mutually exclusive.[77]

---

[74]S. R. R., XXIII (1931), 140, n. 6; S. R. R., XXV (1933), 80, n. 5.

[75]Cf. S. R. R., XXVII (1935), 78-9, n. 5; S. R. R., XXVII (1935), 624, n. 9; S. R. R., XXII (1930), 155, n. 2.

[76]Cf. S. R. R., XXX (1938), 648, n. 3; S. R. R., XXVII (1935), 335, n. 5; S. R. R., XVI (1924), 68, n. 2.

[77]Cf. S. R. R., XXX (1938), 648, n. 3; S. R. R., XXX (1938), 585, n. 1; S. R. R., XXIV (1932), 208, n. 2; S. R. R., XIX (1927), 183, n. 1; S. R. R., III (1911), 237, n. 1.

CHAPTER III

THE "IUS ACCUSANDI" IN CASES OF TOTAL SIMULATION

The Code of Canon Law prohibits all persons other than the Catholic consorts from impugning the validity of a marriage. However, if a Catholic party has been the cause of the impediment he is also estopped from impugning the marriage.[1]

On March 12, 1929, the Pontifical Commission for the Interpretation of the Code declared that the word *impedimenti* of canon 1971, § 1, n. 1, is to be understood as referring not only to impediments in the strict sense (canons 1067-1080), but also to those legal obstacles to marital consent which are described in canons 1081 to 1103.[2] Further elucidation in this matter was supplied by a response of July 17, 1933, in which it was stated that the parties lose the right to impugn the validity of their marriage if they are the culpable cause either of the impediment or of the nullity of the marriage.[3] The same norm was repeated in the Instruction *Provida* of the Sacred Congregation of the Sacraments.[4] Due to the fact that there still remained some obscurity with regard to the expression *causa culpabilis,* the Code Commission clarified the situation to some extent by stating that the parties are deprived of the right of impugning the validity of their marriage only if they were both the direct and the malicious cause of the nullity.[5]

[1]Canon 1971.

[2]*AAS*, XXI (1929), 171.

[3]*AAS*, XXV (1933), 345, ad II.

[4]S. C. de Sacramentis, *Instructio servanda a tribunalibus dioecesanis in pertractandis causis de nullitate matrimoniorum*, 15 aug. 1936, article 37, § 1: "Coniux inhabilis est ad accusandum matrimonium, si fuit ipse causa culpabilis sive impedimenti sive nullitatis matrimonii"—*AAS*, XXVIII (1936), 321.

[5]"Utrum, secundum canonem 1971, § 1, n. 1, et responsum diei iulii 1933 ad II, inhabilis ad accusandum matrimonium habendus sit tantum coniux, qui sive impedimenti sive nullitatis matrimonii causa fuit et directa et dolosa, an etiam coniux qui impedimenti vel nullitatis matrimonii causa exstitit vel indirecta vel doli expers." "R. Affirmative ad primam partem; negative ad secundam."—*AAS*, XXXIV (1942), 241.

According to Canon 2200, § 1, criminal *dolus* presupposes a direct causal act inasmuch as it involves a deliberate will, or, in other words, the result of the act must not only be foreseen but also intended.[6] According to the Code Commission the legal obstacle to the validity must be the direct effect of the person's act if he is to be estopped from impugning the validity of his marriage. It is insufficient that he be only the indirect agent.

In view of the fact that the estoppel is a restriction of a right and at the same time has the nature of a penalty, the conditions for its application are to be strictly interpreted.[7] Nevertheless, ignorance of the declaration of canon 1971, § 1, n. 1, together with that of the official responses, does not afford protection against the loss of the right to impugn.[8]

According to the Response of 1933 and the Instruction *Provida,* a contractant who causes a legal obstacle to the marriage without committing any moral fault is not prevented from impugning the marriage. This declaration is in conformity with canon 2199, which states that there can be no imputability unless either malice *(dolus)* or culpable neglect *(culpa)* be present.[9]

It has been seen in the previous chapter that total simulation signifies that a party has the positive intention of not contracting marriage. The simulator is obviously aware of the fictitious nature of his consent, since he has the deliberate intention of simulating.[10] Hence the person who totally simu-

---

[6]"Dolus heic est deliberata voluntas violandi legem, eique opponitur ex parte intellectus defectus cognitionis et ex parte voluntatis defectus libertatis"—canon 2200, § 1.

[7]Cf. Gasparri, *De Matrimonio*, II, n. 1260; Cappello, *De Sacramentis*, III, n. 878; Doheny, *Canonical Procedure*, I, 88; Francis F. Reh, "Guilt of the Plaintiff in a Marriage Case,"—*The Jurist*, III (1943), 405; Canon 19: "Leges quae poenam statuunt, aut liberum iurium exercitium coarctant,......strictae subsunt interpretationi."

[8]"Nulla ignorantia legum irritantium aut inhabilitantium ab eisdem excusat, nisi aliud expresse dicatur"—Canon 16, § 1.

[9]"Imputabilitas delicti pendet ex dolo delinquentis vel ex eiusdem culpa in ignorantia legis violatae aut in omissione debitae diligentiae; ......"—canon 2199.

[10]S. R. R., XXVIII (1936), 111, n. 11; S. R. R., XXIII (1931), 196, n.

lates matrimonial consent is always the direct cause *sive impedimenti sive nullitatis.* Consequently such a person is presumptively debarred from iupugning on this ground the validity of his marriage before an ecclesiastical tribunal.[11]

According to canon 2200, §2, in the external forum the violation of a law is presumed to have been malicious until the contrary is proved.[12] The onus of proving the fact that he is not the malicious cause of the legal obstacle to the validity of his marriage rests upon the party himself. If he can show that he was acting under the stress of grave fear at the time of the ceremony, in such manner that this fear can be said to have been the reason for the simulation, then he escapes the penalty of estoppel, since the simulation in that case would have been without blame.[13] In a case of doubt as to the simulator's moral guilt his right to impugn the validity of the marriage seems sustainable.[14]

What has been said above is based on the more common interpretation of the phrase, *qui sive impedimenti sive nullitatis matrimonii causa fuit,* which appeared in the response which the Pontifical Commission gave in the year 1942. There is, however, another interpretation.

> "One causes an impediment, not as an isolated fact, but in relation to an actual contract. It is an impediment *only in so far as* it touches the contract, not apart from it. Prior to the contract it is a mere fact, an impediment *in potentia.* Concomitant with the contract it is a real *impedimentum.* Now one can effect this relationship with the contract in two ways: *antecedently* by performing an action, the legal effect of which he allows to perdure to the contract

---

[11]Cf. S. R. R., XXX (1938), 648, n. 3; S. R. R., XXIX (1937), 100, n. 3.

[12]"Posita externa legis violatione, dolus in foro externo praesumntur, donec contrarium probetur."—canon 2200, § 2.

[13]"Simulans, utpote causa culpabilis nullitatis matrimonii, per se non habet ius accusandi matrimonium, sicuti a Pontificia Commissione ad Codicis canones authentice interpretandos declaratum est. Haec tamen dispositio in toto suo rigore non solet applicari, si ex actis, uti in casu, apparet contrahentem metu sibi incusso graviter turbatum et ita ad simulandum adductum fuisee."—S. R. R., XXIX (1937), 100, n. 3.

[14]Cf. canons 2228; 15.

(with perhaps even the underlying fact perduring, as in the case of a defective intention); or *concomitantly* by deliberate misrepresentation, with the result that an existing impediment invalidates the contract. . . . In the first case the legal obstacle invalidates the contract because he (one of the parties) caused it, and therefore its legal effect, to exist; in the second case it invalidates because, though obliged to reveal it, he fraudulently concealed its existence. In both cases the invalidity is due to his action. He is the *impedimenti causa*."[15]

Donnelly, in the article from which the foregoing excerpt is taken, upholds the view that the penalty of estoppel is incurred only by a contractant who fraudulently conceals a legal obstacle to his marriage during the pre-marital investigation. This implies that the penalty can be incurred only when the attempted marriage is contracted *in facie Ecclesiae*. "Consequently any marriage contracted *extra Ecclesiam* would be subject to attack even though the parties entered it in bad faith, aware of their sinful action."[16] However, if this opinion is followed, then in order that a party be permitted to impugn his marriage on the ground that his spouse totally simulated matrimonial consent, it is necessary to show that the innocent party was unaware of the perverse intention of the other. Yet, since the right of attack is in possession, it would be the duty of the defendant or of the defender of the bond to prove that the plaintiff is estopped.

The first opinion is that the response of the Pontifical Commission has reference only to those who are directly the cause of the fact, the legal effect of which is the invalidity of the marriage.[17] Gasparri (1852-1934) who held to this the more common opinion, taught that the spouses who wilfully neglect to seek a dispensation from an impediment which they

---

[15] Francis B. Donnelly, "Fraud and the Estoppel of Canon 1971, § 1, n. 1"—*The Jurist*, VI (1946), 384-5.

[16] *Ibidem*, pp. 398-399.

[17] Cf. Roberti, "De Matrimonii Accusatione,"—*Apollinaris*, (Romae, 1928-), VI (1933), 441-444.

know to exist are not estopped from impugning the marriage.[18] According to his opinion the person who is innocent of the act of simulation would not be estopped. However, it should be noted that Gasparri wrote prior to the last two responses of the Pontifical Commission.

A party who has incurred the penalty of estoppel always retains the right of denouncing his marriage to the Promoter of justice.[19] Since this denunciation is directed towards the public good, it may even be of obligation to do so. A party who is a non-Catholic does not enjoy the right to impugn the validity of his marriage, even though he is innocent of the simulation.[20] However, if there is grave reason why he should be admitted as plaintiff, special recourse may be had to the Holy Office.[21] In any case even a non-Catholic may denounce his marriage to the Promoter of justice. The duties of this official of the ecclesiastical tribunal are beyond the scope of the present study.[22]

Canon 1669, §1, allows several actions to be introduced in the same process, provided that they do not conflict with each other.[23] Consequently a party, in impugning the validity of his marriage, may not claim that it is invalid on the ground of total simulation and at the same time on any other ground of defective consent. Whenever such mutually exclusive grounds are alleged as the cause of the nullity of a particular marriage, they must be considered as alternatives.[24]

18*De Matrimonio*, II, n. 1260.

19Cf. the response of the Pontifical Commission for the interpretation of the Code, of February 17, 1930—*AAS*, XXII (1930), 196.

20S. C. de Sacramentis, *Instructio servanda a tribunalibus dioecesanis in pertractandis causis de nullitate matrimoniorum*, 15 aug. 1936, article 35, § 3—*AAS*, XXVIII (1936), 321.

21*Loc. cit.* Cf. also the response of the Sacred Congregation of the Holy Office of January 27, 1928, ad. I—*AAS*, XX (1928), 75.

22For a study of this subject cf. Glynn, *The Promoter of Justice*, The Catholic University of America Canon Law Studies, n. 101 (Washington, D.C.: Catholic University of America, 1936).

23"Actor pluribus simul actionibus, quae tamen secum ipsae non confligant, sive de eadem re, sive de diversis, reum convenire potest, si aditi tribunalis competentiam non egrediantur."

24Roberti, "Quaestiones quaedam de identificatione actionum ob vitia consensus in causis matrimonialibus."—*Apollinaris*, VI (1933), 105-107. Cf. also S. R. R., XXX (1938), 648, n. 3.

CHAPTER IV

THE GENERAL MODE OF PROOF

A marriage to which one of the contractants has totally simulated consent is null and void. Although the invalidity is known to the simulator, nevertheless, in virtue of the second paragraph of canon 1069, neither party may contract a second marriage until the nullity of the prior one is proved in the external forum.[1]

It is apparent that the question of proof pertains to the external forum alone, since in the forum of conscience *soli confitenti habetur fides.*[2]

Proving fictitious marital consent is among the most difficult of nullity cases, both because consent depends upon an act of the will, which is entirely internal, and because it is always possible that a consort changed his will without giving the least external indication of doing so.[3] The proof of simulation, if it is to be sufficient to justify a declaration of nullity, must overcome not only the general presumption of law in favor of the validity of marriage, as stated in canon 1014, but also the special presumption of canon 1086, §1: *Internus animi consensus semper praesumitur conformis verbis vel signis in celebrando adhibitis.* The basis of the general presumption is the fact that the welfare of marriage affects the public good.[4] The reason for the special presumption is also self-evident: it would be monstrous for the law to presume that what the mouth speaks is not in the heart, since that would be tantamount to presuming the presence of a lie.[5]

---

[1] "Quamvis prius matrimonium sit irritum aut solutum qualibet ex causa, non ideo licet aliud contrahere, antequam de prioris nullitate aut solutione legitime et certo constiterit."—canon 1069, § 2.

[2] Schmalzgrueber, *Ius Ecclesiasticum Universum*, Lib. IV, tit. 1, n. 265. Cf. also Sanchez, *De Matrimonio*, Lib. II, Disp. XLV, n. 2; S. R. R., XXIV (1932), 67, n. 4.

[3] Wanenmacher, *Canonical Evidence in Marriage Cases*, (Philadelphia: Dolphin Press, 1935), n. 151.

[4] S. R. R., XXV (1933), 570-571, n. 4; S. R. R., XXI (1929), 509, n. 3; S. R. R., III (1911), 14, n. 17; Sanchez, *De Matrimonio*, Lib. I, Disp. 18, n. 7.

[5] Sanchez, *De Matrimonio*, Lib. III, Disp. XV, n. 9. The same presumption is expressed in the following axiom of Roman Law: *Nemo existimandus est dixisse quod non mente agitaverit.*—D (33.10).

In marriage cases which involve impediments, proof of nullity is furnished ordinarily through external facts. In cases concerning matrimonial consent on the contrary, the only evidence which is of direct value is that which indicates the actual mind of the parties at the time of the exchange of the consent.[6] Since simulation is constituted through an internal act of the will which is contrary to an external and free act, it is most difficult to prove.[7] Indeed, no direct proof is possible, since only God can see what is in the mind of a man at a particular moment.[8]

Proof that is obtained from documents which are genuine and authentic, or from the sworn testimony of witnesses to facts, is termed direct proof. That which is obtained from presumptions deriving either from the law, or from facts which have been proved, is indirect proof. The latter may be called proof from circumstances or circumstantial evidence.[9] Whenever a direct proof is impossible, the only available method of arriving at the truth is an indirect proof, that is, the obtaining of moral certitude by means of circumstances and presumptions.[10] Since genuine documents can at best furnish proof only of that to which they directly and principally attest,[11] and since witnesses are cited for the purpose of narrating facts, and not for the purpose of expressing opinions or of drawing conclusions,[12] it seems impossible to envisage a case wherein total simulation could become established by means of direct proof. That would imply that the simulator had revealed his true intention at the moment of the act of simulating,

---

[6]Doheny, *Canonical Procedure*, I, 215.

[7]"Simulatus consensus in matrimonio difficilis est probatu."— S. R. R., IV (1912), 405, n. 10. Similar statements are found in practically every case of total simulation contained in the Rota Decisions.

[8]"......for man seeth those things that appear, but the Lord beholdeth the heart."—I Kings, XVI, 7.

[9]James P. Kelly, "Force and Fear Affecting Matrimonial Consent"—*The Jurist*, V (1945), 517.

[10]"Ubi probationes directe haberi non possunt, tunc id quod per circumstantias et praesumptiones probatur, verum esse censetur"—Reiffenstuel, *Ius Canonicum Universum* (5 vols in 7, Parisiis, 1864-1870), Lib. II, tit. XIX, n. 67. Cf. also S. R. R., XXV (1933), 78, n. 2.

[11]Canon 1816.

[12]S. R. R., XXIII (1931), 433, n. 41; S. R. R., XXI (1929), 53, n. 3.

which is repugnant to the notion of simulation. The facts, however, upon which the presumptions are based, do lend themselves to direct proof: indeed they must be established in this manner, since the law prohibits the judge from basing one presumption upon another presumption.[13]

Notwithstanding these considerations the Rota has declared, on at least one occasion, that the possibility of direct proof of simulation is not entirely excluded.

> "Sed haec indirecta probatio non excludit, immo supplet, probationem directam, si haec obtineri possit. Iamvero consensus fictio demonstrari potest directe, si is qui simulavit consensum declaravit ante matrimonii celebrationem se in ineundo coniugio consensum simulaturum esse, ac adiuncta evincunt eum a tali voluntate non recesisse, sed saltem virtualiter in eadem perseverasse: haec tamen omnia idoneis argumentis probari debent."[14]

From the concluding words of this passage it is clear that the declaration of the intention to simulate does not of itself suffice to prove the fact. It must be established that this intention perdured until the moment of the ceremony. But the continuation in existence of an internal act can be established only by means of presumptions—*ac adiuncta evincunt;* this evidently is indirect proof. The meaning of the passage thus seems to be the following: in very evident cases of simulation the majority of the proofs may be concerned with the direct establishment of facts, which then comprise such cogent indications of fictitious consent that the presumption in favor of simulation in the case is almost self-evident. In cases wherein the simulator has, just before the time of the wedding, manifested his intention of simulating, the fact of the simulation may be so evident that the proof may be said to approach the nature of direct proof. Basically, however,

---

[13]"Praesumptiones, quae non statuuntur a iure, iudex ne coniiciat, nisi ex facto certo et determinato, quod cum eo, de quo controversia est, directe cohaereat."—canon 1828. Cf. also Wanenmacher, *Canonical Evidence in Marriage Cases*, n. 393.

[14]S. R. R., XX (1928), 343, n. 3.

it remains indirect, in very consequence of the necessity of employing presumptions.

This interpretation is supported by the circumstances of the case in which the foregoing passage is located. It was a very well-founded case, in which duress had been brought to bear upon a girl in a mission country, and it had been established beyond prudent doubt that she had declared shortly before her marriage that she had intended to deceive the missionary.[15]

Indications (*indicia*) are facts that stand in relation to a presumption in such a manner that reason and experience lead from them to the presumption.[16] A presumption is a probable conjecture as to the existence of something that is uncertain,[17] and it differs from an indication as an effect from a cause.[18]

Enough has been said regarding the various legal presumptions which support the validity of marriage.[19] There are, however, certain presumptions which have been established by past jurisprudence, and which may be termed legal in a broad sense.[20] These provide norms in the formation of personal presumptions (*praesumptiones hominis*), which enable the judge to overcome the more general presumption in favor of the validity of a marriage.[21] The judge is to

---

[15]*Ibidem*, pp. 343-5, nn. 4-5.

[16]Wanenmacher, *Canonical Evidence in Marriage Cases*, n. 385.

[17]Canon 1825.

[18]Wernz-Vidal, *Ius Canonicum*, VI, *De Processibus*, n. 516.

[19]"Praesumptio illa, quae valere facit actum, est regina aliarum praesumptionum ac proinde praesumitur pro validitate actus, donec probetur invalidus"—Reiffenstuel, *Ius Canonicum Universum*, Lib. II, tit. 23, n. 91.

[20]The argument is based on canon 20. Cf. Wanenmacher, *Canonical Evidence in Marriage Cases*, n. 392. The Rota has declared that the jurisprudence of the pre-Code period is still in effect, though many of the norms followed by the Rota today are not found in the Code. Cf. S. R. R., *Buscoducen.*, *Nullitatis Matrimonii*, 7 ian. 1918, coram Revmo. P. D. Guillelmo Sebastianelli, Decano, dec. I, n. 2—S. R. R., X (1918), 2; Griese, *The Marriage Contract and the Procreation of Offspring*, p. 119.

[21]"Generi per speciem derogatur."—Reg. 34, R. J., in VI°.

heed them but it is evident that they do not possess the same force as legal presumptions in the stricter sense.[22]

In the handling of cases of total simulation it has been the practice of the Roman Curia to follow a uniform and constant pattern, and the Sacred Roman Rota even now uses the legal principles and presumptions which has been established by past jurisprudence.[23] The existence of this uniformity is not surprising, since only an indirect proof is available in cases of this type, and hence the very manner of proof may be said to be dictated by the natural law.[24]

The first requisite for a sufficient proof of fictitious consent is the simulator's confession that his consent was not a true one. This confession is the foundation upon which the proof is constructed, for if the simulation is denied, not only must the presumption of canon 1086, § 1, be overcome, but also the denial of the fact by the only person who knows the truth.[25] The *judicial confession* of simulation is therefore the first step in the proof, even though it possesses a mere negative value, and that to which it attests must itself be proved.

The Rota Decisions, however, speak of a confession in a broader sense. It is obviously impossible to establish the existence of an internal intention unless that intention has been revealed in some manner to others.[26] If this revelation is made outside the judicial proceedings, it is referred to as an extra-judicial confession, though it is to be noted that this terminology does not imply that the action confessed is morally reprehensible. It indicates simply the fact of an extra-judicial assertion. In order to possess probative force of any worth, this assertion must have been made before at

[22]Legal presumptions in the strict sense constitute full proof of what is stated in the presumption, and hence the full burden of proof rests with the party who alleges the opposite (canon 1827).

[23]Cf. Wanenmacher, "Some Questions on Vitiated Matrimonial Consent"—*The Ecclesiastical Review (The American Ecclesiastical Review*, Philadelphia, Vols. I—XXXII, 1889-1905; *The Ecclesiastical Review*, Philadelphia, Vols XXXIII-CIX, 1905-1943; *The American Ecclesiastical Review*, Washington, D.C., Vol. CX-, 1944-), CI (1939), 135-136.

[24]S. R. R., XXVI (1934), 452, nn. 4-5.

[25]S. R. R., XXVI (1934), 72, n. 3; S. R. R., XXV (1933), 103, n. 4.

[26]S. R. R., XXVI (1934), 467, n. 3.

least two reliable witnesses, and preferably immediately before or after the celebration of the marriage.[27]

For the simple reason that simulation is a positive human act, it is evident that a simulator must have some motive for giving only a fictitious consent to marriage. Establishing the fact of the existence of such a cause constitutes an essential step of the proof.[28] For determining whether the cause was sufficient to prompt an act of simulation, the particular characteristics of the simulator must be borne in mind. The cause need not have been an objectively grave one, as long as it was sufficient to move the party to simulate rather than to give a true marital consent.

Even though a sufficient cause for simulation is shown to have existed, the actual fact of the simulation remains to be proved. This can be done only by means of circumstantial evidence.

The judge is to base his conjectures and presumptions on the certain and determined facts of the case. The definite facts of the case, which must evidently have a direct connection with the hypothesis that simulation occurred, are to be established by other means than the simple affirmation of the parties.[29] The fact of a simulation can be deduced with moral certitude only when with reference to that fact there are several grave indications which can be explained in no other way than through the fact that the consent was actually fictitious.[30]

It is the task of the judge to determine the probative value of the facts in each case.[31] The arguments must clearly

---

[27]"Actus voluntatis mere internus, ut in casu, nequit evinci nisi indirecte. Ad rem invaluit in fori praxi requirere in primis confessionem simulantis tempore insuspecto, maxime illico post contractum matrimonium, actis aut verbis expressa idoneis testibus, saltem duobus omni exceptione maioribus, qui de ea in iudicio deponere valeant. Confessio enim iudicialis simulantis non attenditur, cum sit ipsa probanda. Et planum est inquirendum esse diligenter in hoc casu in credibilitatem tum actoris tum testium."—S. R. R., XXV (1933), 78, n. 2. Cf. also S. R. R., XXX (1938), 345, n. 2.

[28]S. R. R., XXV (1933), 78, n. 2.

[29]S. R. R., XXIII (1931), 294, n. 4.

[30]S. R. R., XXVI (1934), 73, n. 5.

[31]S. R. R., XXVI (1934), 673, n. 4.

prove simulation, and not make it merely probable.[32] All the circumstances connected with the marriage are to be considered, as well as what preceded and what followed the ceremony. There are certain circumstances which, if they exist in a particular case, are considered by the Rota as graver indications of simulation than others. These will be treated in the chapter dealing with the circumstantial evidence.[33]

---

[32]S. R. R., XXV (1933), 443, n. 2.

[33]Re the general mode of proving simulation (confession, cause, circumstances), cf. also: Gasparri, *De Matrimonio*, II, n. 818; Wernz-Vidal, *Ius Matrimoniale*, n. 460; Chelodi, *De Matrimonio*, n. 115; Payen, *De Matrimonio*, II, n. 1672; Cappello, *De Sacramentis*, III, n. 603; Ayrinhac, *Marriage Legislation*, n. 205; Coronata, *De Sacramentis*, III, n. 460.

CHAPTER V

THE JUDICIAL CONFESSION OF SIMULATION

Article 117 of the Instruction *Provida* employs the word deposition to refer to the statements which are made by a party before the judge.[1] In cases of total simulation this word is applicable to any statements made by the parties regardless of whether a simulation is or is not confessed.

According to canon 1750, a judicial confession is an oral or written statement which is made by one party against his own claims and in favor of the other party. It may be elicited either spontaneously or as a result of the questioning of the judge, but to merit the name *judicial* it must be made in the presence of the judge.[2] The following canon states that in matters which are merely of private interest the judicial confession of one of the parties, provided that it is freely and deliberately made, relieves the other party of the burden of proof.[3]

It is evident that a judicial confession does not possess this full probative value in matrimonial cases, since every marriage pertains to the public good — *Quia partes nequeunt disponere de publico bono.*[4] In other than matrimonial cases a confession jeopardizes the position of the person confessing, whereas in marriage cases such a confession is directed towards something that is frequently desired equally by both

---

[1]S. C. de Sacramentis, *Instructio servanda a tribunalibus dioecesanis in pertractandis causis de nullitate matrimoniorum*, 15 aug. 1936, article 117: "Depositio iudicialis coniugum non est apta ad probationem contra valorem matrimonii constituendam."—*AAS*, XXVIII (1936), 337.

[2]"Assertio de aliquo facto, in scriptis aut oretenus ab una parte contra se et pro adversario coram iudice, sive sponte, sive iudice interrogante peracta, dicitur confessio iudicialis."—canon 1750.

[3]"Si agatur de negotio aliquo privato et in causa non sit bonum publicum, confessio iudicialis unius partis, dummodo libere et considerate facta, relevat alteram ab onere probandi."—canon 1751.

[4]Roberti, *De Processibus* (2 vols., Romae: Apud Aedes Facultatis Iuridicae ad S. Apollinaris, 1926), II, 36. Cf. also S. R. R., XXVIII (1936), 614-615, n. 16; S. R. R., XXV (1933), 570-571, n. 4.

parties, namely, the obtaining of a declaration of nullity. The reason why the presumption in favor of validity overrules the sworn confession of simulation is the very obvious one that otherwise the door would be open to divorce and adultery at the mere allegation of the consorts.[5]

In cases wherein a marriage has been impugned on the ground of simulation, an additional reason why the unsupported confession of the consorts is inacceptable as proof of the fact is provided by the special presumption of law stated in canon 1086, § 1. External words constitute signs of what is internally willed. Since a sign connotes definite presumptions or conjectures, the presumption to be drawn from the fact that a person has apparently manifested matrimonial consent is that there was a harmony between the internal will and that which was expressed.[6]

This presumption which militates against believing a confession of simulation was stated in the Gregorian Decretals, and it was amply commented upon by pre-Code authors.[7] It has likewise been upheld in the constant jurisprudence of the Rota.[8] Consequently article 117 of the 1936 Instruction

---

[5] S. R. R., XXI (1929), 509, n. 3.

[6] "In foro externo non stare intentioni contrahentium, eo quod ea Ecclesiam lateat, sed communi verborum intelligentiae, cogeturque uterque in eo sensu verba retinere, quem communiter recte intelligentibus generare solent."—Sanchez, *De Matrimonio*, Lib. I, Disp. XVIII, n. 4. Cf. Gonzales-Tellez, *Commentaria*, Lib. IV, tit. I, cap. 26; Pichler, *Epitome Iuris Canonici* (2 vols. Venetiis, 1755), Lib. IV, tit. 1, n. 3.

[7] "......quum nimis indignum sit iuxta legitimas sanctiones, ut, quod sua quisque voce dilucide protestatus est, id in eundem casum proprio valeat testimonio infirmare."—c. 10, X, *de probationibus*, II, 19. This quotation was borrowed from the Code of Justinian; C. (4.30) 13. Cf. Sanchez, *De Matrimonio*, Lib. II, Disp. XLV, n. 2; Laymann, *Theologia Moralis*, Lib. V, Tract. X, Pars. II, cap. 6, n. 2; Schmalzgrueber, *Ius Ecclesiasticum Universum*, Lib. IV, tit. I, n. 266; D'Annibale, *Summula Theologiae Moralis* (3 ed., 3 vols., Romae 1888-1892), n. 412, nota 45.

[8] "Itaque ad probandum non satis est affirmatio, licet iurata, simulantis, neque utriusque partis; quamvis simulantis confessio cum aliis probationibus requiratur, ut pateat dissensus qui in corde latuerit: ......"—S. R. R., XXIII (1931), 293, n. 4. Cf. also, S. R. R., XXVIII (1936), 614-615, n. 16; S. R. R., XXVII (1935), 622, n. 4; S. R. R., XXVI (1934), 673, n. 3; S. R. R., XXV (1933), 78, n. 2; S. R. R., XXIV (1932), 67, n. 4; S. R. R., XXIII (1931), 78-79, n. 11; S. R. R., XXII (1930), 377, n. 10; S. R. R., XIX (1927), 193, n. 2; S. R. R., VI (1914), 329, n. 12; S. R. R., IV (1912), 461, n. 6.

states that the judicial deposition of the consorts is not admissible as proof against the validity of a marriage.

Notwithstanding its lack of probative value, the judicial confession is of capital importance in all cases which involve matrimonial consent, and especially in cases of simulation.[9] The apparent manifestation of consent that is offered at the time of the marriage ceremony indicates that the party has the intention of contracting marriage. If the person is simulating consent, the fact that he is doing so is directly known by none other than himself.[10]

Simulation can be proved in the external forum solely by means of the outward effects which it causes. In other words, only when a person's conduct and external behavior can be explained in no other way than by the fact that his marital consent was not a true one can the existence of simulation be said to be proved. The knowledge of the fact of simulation that is had by other persons can never be more than indirect, whereas the simulator's knowledge is direct and immediate.[11]

When the person who is accused of simulation denies the fact, a serious obstacle to the proof is created, for in this case all the presumptions which are opposed to the acceptance of a confession of simulation derive further support from the fact of the denial, and the evidence must prove the fact of simulation so clearly that the denial is shown to have been a falsehood.[12] In several instances the Rota has declared the invalidity of marriage on the ground of total simulation in spite of the fact that there had been no judicial confession by the simulator. However, these decisions have always been based upon evidence that was sufficient to account for the person's contumacy or false denial.[13]

A confession of simulation is therefore required as a rule if the non-consent or dissent which was hidden in the heart at the

[9]Doheny, *Canonical Procedure*, I, 215.
[10]S. R. R., XVIII (1926), 253-254, n. 4.
[11]S. R. R., XX (1928), 343, n. 3.
[12]Cf. S. R. R., XXVIII (1936), 129-134; S. R. R., XXVI (1934), 73, n. 7; S R. R., IV (1912), 405, n. 10.
[13]Cf. S. R. R., XXVII (1935), 522-3, nn. 6-7; S. R. R., XVIII (1926), 35, n. 4; S. R. R., XVI (1924), 157 n. 7; S. R. R., XV (1923), 228, n. 12; S. R. R., XI (1919), 36-45; S. R. R., VII (1915), 195, n. 1; S. R. R., III (1911), 16-29; 325-331; 346-351; 460-472.

time of the wedding is to be made manifest.[14] The confession of simulation is thus the foundation upon which the proof is constructed, and the greater the credence that can be attached to it, the more firm will be the basis for the proof.[15]

Although the judicial confession is of no positive probative value in the establishment of the fact of simulation, it would nevertheless constitute a grave omission to neglect a cautious examination of the party's deposition. A confession of simulation is never to be accepted lightly. Not only is there ever present the danger that the person is fraudulently accusing himself of simulation in order to liberate himself from an unhappy marriage, but it also is not of infrequent occurrence that a person in good faith is led into error by his desire to be free of his spouse. A marital troth pledged to a person whom one does not love may easily be confused with total simulation.[16]

The party who makes a judicial confession of fictitious matrimonial consent must reveal by his confession that he is, and has always been, fully aware of his simulation. If it become apparent that his marital consent had been merely uncertain, or given reluctantly, the truth of the matter may be that he has simulated the confession, and not the consent.[17] In determining

---

[14] S. R. R., XXII (1930), 377, n. 10.

[15] "Quae assertio licet non habeat vim probandi, tamen quo maior est credibilitas affirmantis, eo solidius fundamentum habetur pro probando ipso facto simulationis."—S. R. R., XXIII (1931), 293, n. 4. Cf. S. R. R., XXIII (1931), 380, n. 2.

[16] Cf. S. R. R., XXVII (1935), 543, n. 4.

[17] "At eius confessio, si qua habetur, caute aestimanda est. Etenim nom solum est periculum, quominus praetensus simulans hodie in iudicio perperam se accuset simulationis, ad iugium infausti matrimonii excutiendum, sed non raro etiam aliquis, ob desiderium sese liberandi a coniuge, bona fide inducitur in errorem. Sene, facile consensus absque amore datus confunditur cum consensu proprie simulato. Attamen non omnis, qui amorem fingit, eo ipso etiam ipsum consensum simulat. Immo e contrario is, qui v. g. in conscientia se obligatum putat ad contrahendum cum sponsa non amplius amata, solet verum et sincerum consensum elicere, neque de simulando cogitare. Postuma autem persuasio contrahentis, acquisita demum post colloquia cum advocatis habita, de ficto consensu praestito, omnino negligenda est. Siquidem vera fictio consensus ignorari nequit ab eo, qui hoc delictum committit, quippe qui postivum voluntatis actum cantrarium ponere debet, ut destruat effectum verborum consensum matrimonialem experimentium. Qui proinde in iudicio sibi adscribit simulationem consensus, is necessario in contrahendo sibi conscius esse debuit suae fictionis; secus nunc fingit, non vero prius."— S. R. R., XXVIII (1936), 101, n. 3.

the value of the judicial confession the judge must examine not only the character of the party and the confirmation afforded the confession by the various testimonies and other evidence, but also the intrinsic sufficiency of the confession itself.

The more trustworthy the consort, the greater also the credence that can be allotted to his confession of simulation. The unlikelihood of perjury in a particular case will be indicated to a greater or less extent by the consort's honesty, fidelity to his religious duties, and general moral probity.[18] When the alleged simulation was due to malicious intent, the integrity of the offender can well be called into question to such an extent that he cannot be relied upon even under oath.[19] However, if subsequent to the simulation but prior to the confession the party has been genuinely converted to the true faith, or at least has resumed the fervent practice of religion, there would be an indication that his confession merits greater credence.[20] It may be necessary to summon special character witnesses in order to establish the trustworthiness of the parties, though frequently the characters of the consorts become well known to the court by means of subsequent testimonies.

It sometimes happens that a party contradicts in a later deposition what he has previously stated in his judicial confession. In one case that had been appealed to the Rota from Montreal, the defendant claimed that during the wedding ceremony he had verbally denied consenting to the marriage, though at the same time he had nodded his head affirmatively. The only definite confirmation of this statement was provided by the plaintiff. A principal factor that led to the rejection of the

---

[18]For examples wherein the judicial confession was accorded little credence, principally because of the character of the alleged simulator, cf.: S. R. R., XXX (1938), 587, n. 4; S. R. R., XXIX (1937), 155, n. 13; S. R. R., XXVII (1935), 552, n. 3; S. R. R., XXIV (1932), 155, n. 8; S. R. R., XXI (1929), 513, n. 8; S. R. R., XVIII (1926), 264, n. 6; S. R. R., VIII (1916), 199-200, n. 5; S. R. R., IV (1912), 466, n. 18; S. R. R., II (1910), 320-322, n. 9. Examples in which a person's upright character lent support to his claim that he had simulated consent: S. R. R., XVII (1935), 529, n. 17; S. R. R., XXIII (1931), 77, n. 9.

[19]Doheny, *Canonical Procedure*, I, 566.

[20]S. R. R., XX (1928), 393-394, n. 4; Sanchez, *De Matrimonio*, Lib. II, Disp. XLV, n. 9.

judicial confession by the Rota was the discrepancy in the man's testimony regarding the number of interrogations that had been put to him during the ceremony.[21]

Although the unsupported statements of the parties are never sufficient to warrant a declaration of nullity, the case is nevertheless illustrative of the fact that, when the evidence in a particular instance is doubtfully sufficient, the presence of contradictions in the depositions, or the presence of falsehood therein, serves at least to expedite a decision upholding the validity of the marriage.[22] A similar lack of credence would accompany a party's deposition if the self-contradiction is in evidence from statements made by him outside his judicial confession, or if it is perceived that he has deliberately concealed certain facts of the case.[23]

Certain persons have attempted to obtain dispensations from their marriages which they alleged to be non-consummated, and only after receiving an unfavorable decision on this score did they impugn the validity of their marriages on the ground of total simulation. Such a procedure may well indicate the bad faith of the parties, since it appears that they came to a knowledge of the invalidity of their marriage at a time that is suspect.[24]

It may happen that the possibility of total simulation in a particular case is excluded by the deposition of the same consort who confessed to having feigned consent. Any statement of the party to the effect that, in spite of his antipathy toward the marriage, he nevertheless intended to establish a home or to be faithful to the marital obligations, is of course a refutation of simulation.[25]

In a certain case the plaintiff stated that she had been induced to marry under duress. She claimed that she had never

---

[21]S. R. R., XXI (1929), 173-4 n,n. 4-5.

[22]For other examples of depositions that were self contradictory, cf.: S. R. R., XXX (1938), 587, n. 4; S. R. R., XXVI (1934), 414, n. 11.

[23]Cf. S. R. R., XXI (1929), 513, n. 8.

[24]Cf. S. R. R., XXIII (1931), 226-228, nn. 6-9; S. R. R., XVIII (1926), 265-6, n. 9.

[25]S. R. R., XXI (1929), 208, n. 4; S. R. R., XII (1920), 48-49, n. 3.

interiorly consented to the marriage, and being under compulsion to submit to the ceremony, she had entered the marriage not of her own will but in a sheer sense of obedience and gratitude. She confessed, however, that at the time of the wedding she had had the intention of establishing a home and of being faithful to her duties as a spouse, hoping that her aversion for the man would subsequently disappear. The Rota decreed that when a plaintiff who accuses himself of simulation makes a statement such as this, it becomes absolutely impossible to prove total simulation in the case.[26]

In all cases in which force and fear is alleged as a cause of total simulation, a confession by the consort that he actually consented to the marriage precludes the possibility of a declaration of nullity on this ground.[27] The plaintiff who impugns his marriage on the ground of force and fear and simultaneously on the ground of total simulation weakens his case:[28] of the two causes of invalidity, the existence of total simulation seems to be the more difficult to prove.[29]

A Rota decision of the year 1931 affords an excellent illustration of the distinction between the case of total simulation and that of the absence of consent. The plaintiff, who had claimed that he totally simulated consent, spoke the following words in a subsequent session of the trial:

> "During the wedding I didn't even think of giving a fictitious consent; indeed I wasn't thinking of anything, my mind was far away. . . . .The moment of the ceremony was a horrible one for me. . . .I was a dazed, senseless person. . . .In pronouncing the words of consent, I didn't know what I was doing, and I say it again a thousand times, if necessary, and I swear to it,. . . . .I was insensible, passive, not thinking of what I was saying; I would have

---

[26]"Quod actrix nec asseruit nec vindicat, quod immo aperte excludit, nequit profecto probari per testes."—S. R. R., XVII (1925), 177, n. 6.

[27]S. R. R., XXIV (1932), 208, n. 2.

[28]S. R. R., XXVII (1935), 624, n. 9.

[29]Cf. S. R. R., V (1913), 286, n. 5 for a case in which it was doubtful whether the party had actually consented to the marriage: the declaration of nullity was on the ground of force and fear.

answered "yes" or "no" automatically without knowing what I was saying."[30]

The observations made by the Rota in this case make it clear that cases of this nature do not comprise instances of total simulation, for which the positive intention of not contracting must be present. It seems that the only ground upon which marriages contracted in such circumstances should be impugned is that of the absence of consent. As has been remarked above, the person who accuses himself of a total simulation and at the same time of a lack of consent contradicts himself and thus weakens his case.[31] For a declaration of nullity on the ground of the absence of consent, it must be established not only that the party did not have an actual intention of marrying, but also that he did not even possess a virtual intention of doing so. The simple defect of an actual intention to marry does not affect the validity of the contract.[32]

The same self-contradiction is present in a judicial confession when a party claims that he totally simulated consent and that he simultaneously entertained a positive intention contrary to one of the blessings of marriage.[33] Even though the party who now accuses himself of total simulation has confessed partial simulation in a previous instance only, he nevertheless appears to be seeking a declaration of the nullity of his marriage regardless of the grounds.[34] A more or less practical norm for distinguishing between the two types of simulation is presented in the following case.

A certain man impugned the validity of his marriage on the ground that his wife had simulated her consent to the marriage.

---

[30]"Lors du mariage, je n'ai même pas pensé à donner un consentement fictif, je ne pensais à rien, j'étais complètement absent. . . Le moment de la cérémonie fut pour moi horrible. . . .J'étais un homme étourdi, inconscient. . . .En prononçant la formule du consentement, je le répète mille fois, s'il le faut, et je le jure, je ne savais pas ce que je faisais. . . J'étais sans réflexe, je me laissais faire, je ne pensais pas à ce que je disais; j'aurais répondu oui ou non machinalement, sans savoir ce que je disais."—S. R. R., XXIII (1931), 195-196, n. 5.

[31]S. R. R., XXVII (1935), 624, n. 9.

[32]S. R. R., XXIII (1931), 196, n. 7.

[33]Cf. S. R. R., XXIII (1931), 140-141, nn. 5-7.

[34]Cf. S. R. R., XXV (1933), 80, n. 5; S. R. R., XXII (1930), 386, n. 3.

Both total and partial simulation were mentioned in the *libellus*. The woman admitted in court that she had desired to marry the plaintiff solely because the civil status conferred through the marriage would provide her with greater freedom to continue her sinful relations with her lover. She claimed that she had had no intention of obliging herself to the duties of the married state. In virtue of this deposition, the Rota determined that this was not a case of total, but rather of partial simulation, and subsequently the marriage was declared null on the ground of the exclusion of the blessing of offspring.[35]

A person who partially simulates marital consent has at least the intention of acquiring a certain status by marrying, even though that status does not possess all the essential features or obligations of matrimony. On the contrary, the party who has the positive intention of not contracting marriage necessarily regards the matrimonial contract as devoid of any real effect, and hence as a mere formality.[36]

An indication that total simulation is absent in a particular case may be provided by the presence of yet another circumstance. In another case before the Rota, both parties had confessed that they had considered their marriage as a free union, that they had submitted to the ceremony solely to please the plaintiff's mother, but that they themselves considered it as devoid of any real effect. The Rota rejected the ground of total simulation, not only because of the failure to prove that a sufficient cause of simulation had existed, but also because conditions which were contrary to the blessings of offspring and sacramental stability had been attached to the consent. The marriage was declared null because of a condition contrary to the essential property of indissolubility.[37]

The proof of the fact of total simulation in a particular case is accomplished only when the existence of a sufficient cause of the simulation has been established, and at the same

---

35S. R. R., XV (1923), 168, n. 6.

36A case wherein the intention of a non-Catholic to marry only according to the civil law was interpreted as simple error, and not as simulation, is found in S. R. R., XXV (1933), 574, n. 10.

37S. R. R., XV (1923), 144, n. 6.

time the presence of certain facts and circumstances can be explained only as the effects of a feigned consent. In some Rota cases the judicial confession has been technically adequate, but the invalidity of the marriages in question has remained unproved because of the lack of sufficient evidence.[38]

As a summary of the foregoing it may be stated that although a judicial confession does not prove the fact of simulation, the absence of such a confession produces a damaging effect on the cause of the plaintiff. This is true especially when the plaintiff accuses himself of the simulation, for in this case any admission by the party that he regarded himself as married for a while, or that he attached a condition to his consent, or that he consented under duress, renders the proof of total simulation impossible. When the simulation is attributed to the defendant, and his confession indicates the presence of any of these contrary elements, then it is not considered as a confession at all, for it is tantamount to a denial.[39] A denial of simulation by the accused person necessitates a stronger proof.[40]

Although the force of a denial is great, it would nevertheless be an injustice to dismiss a case simply for the reason that the defendant has denied the simulation; this he may have done precisely to thwart the plaintiff's desires.[41] A denial of simulation, like a confession thereof, is to be evaluated in the light of a consideration of the person's character, of his past conduct, of his feelings for the other party, and of the possible motives that may have prompted his denial.[42] Two of the more common motives that have induced persons to deny the fact that they simu-

---

[38]Cf. S. R. R., XXII (1930), 194-5, nn. 7-8; S. R. R., XIX (1927), 190, n. 16; S. R. R., XVI (1924), 314, n. 4; S. R. R., II (1910), 27, n. 9.

[39]Cf. S. R. R., XXV (1933), 472, n. 20.

[40]The following examples represent cases wherein the proof was regarded as insufficient to overcome the denial of simulation by the defendant: S. R. R., XXX (1938), 347, n. 5; S. R. R., XXIX (1937), 664, n. 3; S. R. R., XXVIII (1936), 129-134; S. R. R., XXVI (1934), 73, n. 7; S. R. R., XXVI (1934), 675, n. 8; S. R. R., XXV (1933), 249-250, n. 15; S. R. R., XX (1928), 246, n. 3; S. R. R., XVII (1925), 375-6, n. 4; S. R. R., XV (1923), 32-3, n. 5; S. R. R., XII (1920), 48-9, n. 3; S. R. R., IV (1912), 405, n. 10.

[41]S. R. R., XXII (1930), 57, n. 5.

[42]Cf. S. R. R., XXVIII (1936), 130-131, nn. 3-4; S. R. R., XXVII (1935), 375, n. 4.

lated consent are a vehement dislike for the other party and the desire for financial betterment to be derived from the continuance or resumption of the conjugal life.[43]

Contumacy on the part of the supposed simulator is obviously not the equivalent of a denial of the simulation. Yet the non-appearance in court of the accused constitutes an obstacle to the cause of the plaintiff, and there have been many cases in which such contumacy has been a contributing factor in bringing about an unfavorable decision.[44] However, when the accused fails to respond to the citation, it may be that the extra-judicial confession and other circumstances in the case can supply for the defect of the judicial confession.[45]

The Rota has declared nullity in many cases in spite of the simulator's contumacy, but the evidence has always been such as to offer a sufficient explanation for the refusal to respond to the citation.[46] The most frequent cause of contumacy in the Rota cases which treat of total simulation is the complete indifference or the antipathy of the person towards the other party or towards the Church.[47]

---

[43]Cf. S. R. R., XXIX (1937), 681, n. 11; S. R. R., XXVII (1935), 522-523, nn. 6-7; S. R. R., XXVI (1934), 167-168, n. 4; S. R. R., XVII (1925), 375-6, n. 4; S. R. R., XVI (1924), 157, n. 7; S. R. R., XV (1923), 228, n. 12; S. R. R., IV (1912), 405, n. 9.

[44]Cf. S. R. R., XXVII (1935), 551-555; S. R. R., XXVI (1934), 408-417; S. R. R., XXI (1929), 547-552, especially 549, nn. 6-7.

[45]"Si autem is qui dicitur consensum simulasse, non comparuerit aut dolo negaverit simulationem, defectui confessionis iudicialis suppleri potest, puta per eiusdem confessionem extraiudicialem ac per alia indicia perspicua."—S. R. R., XXIX (1937), 664, n. 3.

[46]Cf. S. R. R., XVIII (1926), 35, n. 4; S. R. R., XI (1919), 36-45; S. R. R., VII (1915), 195, n. 1; S. R. R., III (1911), 325-331; S. R. R., III (1911), 346-352.

[47]Cf., e. g., S. R. R., III (1911), 465-466, nn. 11-12.

CHAPTER VI

THE EXTRA-JUDICIAL CONFESSION OF SIMULATION

An extra-judicial confession, according to canon 1753, is a confession made by a party to his adversary or to others outside of the court. The same canon declares that when such a confession is referred to the court it pertains to the office of the judge to determine its value in view of all the circumstances of the case.[1]

Article 116 of the Instruction *Provida* states that the extra-judicial confession of a consort which impugns the validity of his marriage and which was made before the wedding, or even after it, but at a time that is not suspect, should be considered by the judge as corroborative evidence.[2]

The nature of simulation indicates the necessity of some revelation by the party of his actual intention if the fact of the simulation is to be proved in the external forum.[3] As has been indicated, the word *confession* does not necessarily convey the notion of moral guilt, for it is quite possible that the influence of force and fear may preclude all moral imputability for the action.

An extra-judicial confession may take the form of an oral statement or it may be made in writing. It may be addressed to the other consort or to relatives, friends, acquaintances and the

---

1 "Confessio sive scriptis, sive oretenus, ipsimet adversario aut aliis extra iudicium facta, dicitur extraiudicialis: eaque in iudicium deducta, iudicis est, perpensis omnibus rerum adiiunctis, aestimare quanti facienda sit."—canon 1753.

2 "Confessio extraiudicialis coniugis, quae adversus matrimonii valorem pugnet, prolata ante matrimonium contractum, vel post matrimonium, sed tempore non suspecto, probationis adminiculum constituit a iudice recte aestimandum."—*AAS*, XXVIII (1936), 321.

3 "Cum autem dissensus in corde lateat, via ad eum probandum aperitur per affirmationem eius qui dicitur consensum simulasse:. . . ."—S. R. R., XXX (1938), 345, n. 2.

like. Moreover, the term is not confined to a revelation of intention made in words alone. Any manifestation of the fact that a fictitious consent was given be it only by acts or deeds, may rightly be considered an extra-judicial confession.[4] However, since external acts and conduct can be more suitably treated under the general heading of circumstances, the present chapter will be confined to a consideration of the verbal extra-judicial confession.

In evaluating the alleged extra-judicial assertions of a consort who has been accused of simulating matrimonial consent, the judge considers them under three aspects, namely: their authenticity, the time at which they were made, and their meaning in themselves and in relation to the circumstances in which they were spoken.

In the first place, it is necessary to establish the fact that the alleged statements were actually made by the person to whom they are attributed. This is done in the same manner as is the establishment of any fact, that is, by means of documentary and especially by means of testimonial evidence. If the statements are contained in written documents (e.g., private letters), these documents are presented to the court and the usual norms for the evaluation of documents are observed. More frequently statements of this nature are made in an oral fashion, and thus the principal if not the sole way of establishing the fact is by means of testimonial evidence. The witnesses should declare, in so far as they are able, the actual words spoken by the party, the persons addressed, the circumstances accompanying the statements, and only secondarily their own personal interpretations of what was spoken.

Without the fact of an extra-judicial confession of simulation the other circumstances of a case are usually of little value in furnishing proof for the fact of fictitious consent, and the Rota has rejected many cases precisely because of the absence of

---

[4] S. R. R., XXVI (1934), 467, n. 3; S. R. R., XXV (1933), 78, n. 2; S. R. R., XXV (1933), 443, n. 2.

any admission of an intention of simulating, or at least for the reason that such an admission was insufficiently proved.[5]

In one instance, however, the Rota declared a marriage null in spite of the fact that there had been only one witness who had heard the defendant state that she did not intend to contract a true marriage.[6] In this case the presence of two probable motives for her simulation and her aversion towards the other party both before and after the ceremony provided very grave indications that her marital consent was fictitious.[7]

If the statements of the party are to possess corroborative value, there is necessarily postulated the fact that they were made at a time that is not suspect.[8] The only definition of *tempus non suspectum* that has appeared in modern canonical legislation is found in the Decree *Catholica Doctrina* of the Sacred Congregation of the Sacraments of the year 1923.[9] There it is defined as *that time when there was not even a thought of introducing the question, and there were no other reasons for concealing the truth or stating a falsehood.*[10]

This definition was given as having reference to cases which are concerned with the proof of the non-consummation of marriages, but it can also be applied to most nullity cases. Statements made by the consorts, or letters written by them at a time when they had no intention of impugning the validity of their marriage, can usually be accepted as representing the truth. On the other hand, all statements, writings and depositions of the con-

5Cf. S. R. R., XXX (1938), 346, n. 4; S. R. R., XXX (1938), 588, n. 5; S. R. R., XXIX (1937), 529-530, n. 6; S. R. R., XXVII (1935), 543, n. 4; S. R. R., XXVI (1934), 78, n. 17; S. R. R., XXVI (1934), 167-8, n. 4; S. R. R., XXV (1933), 78-9, n. 3; S. R. R., XXV (1933), 241-252; S. R. R., XXII (1930), 197, n. 12; S. R. R., XVII (1925), 376, n. 6; S. R. R., IV (1912), 405, n. 10.

6S. R. R., XI (1919), 36-45.

7*Ibidem*, pp. 44-45, nn. 10-11.

8S. C. de sacramentis, instr. *Provida*, 1936, art. 116—*AAS*, XXVIII (1936), 337; S. R. R., XXVIII (1936), 614, n. 16.

9Doheny, *Canonical Procedure*, II, 325.

10S. C. de Sacramentis, decr., *Regulae Servandae in Processibus super Matrimonio Rato et non Consummato*, 7 maii, 1923, n. 70: "Causam enim valde iuvant partium confessiones extraiudiciales tempore non suspecto prolatae; eo nempe tempore, quando de hac quaestione introducenda ne cogitabatur quidem, nec aliae suberant rationes veritatem occultandi aut falsum proferendi."—*AAS*, XV (1923), 389.

sorts and interested parties which are made only after the possibility of a declaration of nullity has been discovered are ordinarily to be considered as having been made *tempore suspecto.*[11]

As can readily be seen, this definition does not apply in every aspect to cases of total simulation. The person who totally simulates matrimonial consent is fully aware of his act, and hence also of the consequent nullity of his marriage.[12] Thus it could quite easily happen that at every moment the simulator was fully aware of the possibility of a declaration of nullity. Indeed, some persons have prepared documents before the ceremony for the very purpose of proving the simulation before the court at a subsequent date.[13]

The strict insistence on the above given definition of *tempus suspectum* could only lead to the conclusion that in most instances of total simulation there is no *tempus non suspectum.* This patent absurdity is avoided if only the latter part of the above definition is considered as having force in cases of total simulation. *Tempus non suspectum* in these cases refers to that period of time when no reasons existed which would have urged a consort to state a falsehood by declaring that his consent was fictitious.

The usual motive that prompts persons to declare untruthfully that they have simulated marital consent is the desire to be free of an unhappy marriage bond. But this desire is also present in a true case of total simulation: indeed the essence of total simulation implies that the will is adverse to even contracting the hated marriage. What then is the difference in fact between the case of total simulation and one that is now falsely alleged to have been such?

The distinguishing characteristics of total simulation is that at no time, either before, during, or after marriage, did the simulator wish a true conjugal union. In the case that is

---

[11]Doheny, *loc. cit.*

[12]The one exception to this statement is, as has been seen, the case wherein the cause of the simulation was force and fear, and the party was so distracted during the ceremony that he is unable afterwards to say whether or not he consented to the marriage.

[13]Cf. S. R. R., XXIX (1937), 104-5, n. 9; *Fontes*, 3282.

falsely alleged as simulation, the consort at one time, at least before, during, and shortly after the ceremony, wished to contract a true marriage, and only after some period of time did he become weary of the union and begin to cherish the hope of dissolving it. Consequently a confession of fictitious consent that was made before, during, or shortly after the ceremony, must be regarded as meriting greater credence for the very reason that it was made at a time that was not suspect.[14] The length of the *tempus non suspectum* varies in each particular case.

Much of the jurisprudence of the Sacred Roman Rota has been deduced from the *Instructio Austriaca* of Cardinal Rauscher (1797-1875). The following quotation is taken from this Instruction:

> "A confession which the consorts make during the progress of the trial itself, or which they made at any earlier time after their contraction of the marriage that is being impugned, lacks all force when it militates against the validity of the marriage."[15]

In commenting upon this general norm, the Rota has remarked that it is to be observed with certain moderation. It is true that the confession of the consorts is considered as suspect by the law; yet, if the circumstances are such that it is apparent that no foundation for this suspicion actually exists, then, although the confession never provides full proof of the fact, it may nevertheless supply corroborative evidence of no little worth.

A confession of the consort is to be heeded particularly in those cases which involve the internal intention of a person,

---

[14]"Maximi autem momenti coniectura habetur, si quis illico et incontinenti post initum matrimonium, verbis vel factis aperiat se ficte consensisse."—S. R. R., XXI (1929), 146, n. 5. Cf. also S. R. R., XXVI (1934), 4, n. 3; S. R. R., XXVI (1934), 674, n. 4; S. R. R., XXIII (1931), 300, n. 15.

[15]Instructio pro iudiciis ecclesiasticis quoad causas matrimoniales, § 148—*Acta et Decreta Sacrorum Conciliorum Recentiorum, Collectio Lacensis* (7 vols., Friburgi Brisgoviae, 1870-1890), V, 1305. The translation is furnished by the present writer. Cf. Doheny, *Canonical Procedure*, I, 214.

since these can hardly be proved without the aid of such a confession.[16] Extra-judicial assertions of simulation that have been made at a time that is suspect are usually of no probative value whatsoever, yet in certain instances they may provide adminicular proof.[17]

When the alleged extra-judicial confession has been established as authentic, and when it has also been proved that it was made at a time that is not suspect, there still remains the task of determining its significance as an indication of the party's intention. What has been stated regarding the interpretation of the judicial confession has application also to the extra-judicial assertion. It should be remembered that it is very difficult to determine a person's true intention unless the words which were used when the intention was expressed are brought to light in the course of the judicial proceedings.

The confession of the simulation must have been of such nature that it was made apparent to the witnesses that the party was fully aware that his marriage was not a true one. A certain person once claimed that he married only to overcome boredom, that he intended simply to do what everyone else does! This certainly was no indication that there had been a restriction in his matrimonial consent.[18] Such a statement as: "In my heart I didn't want this marriage," does not of itself indicate the absence of a true marital consent.[19]

Similarly the expression "to give marriage a try" (*essayer*

---

[16]S. R. R., XXVI (1934), 758, n. 2. Cf. Sanchez, *De Matrimonio*, Lib. II, Disp. XLV, n. 13.

[17]Cf. S. R. R., XXIX (1937), 100-104, nn. 4-9. The following cases provide examples in which the Rota considered assertions of simulation as valueless in view of the point of time at which they had been made: S. R. R., XXIX (1937). 315, n. 3; S. R. R., XXVIII (1936), 12, n. 14; S. R. R., XXVIII (1936), 12, n. 14; S. R. R., XXVII (1935), 706, n. 5; S. R. R., XXVI (1934), 676, n. 8; S. R. R., XXIII (1931), 297, n. 8; S. R. R., XVI (1924), 317, n. 7; S. R. R., XII (1920), 53, n. 8; S. R. R., VI (1914), 329, n. 12.

[18]S. R. R., XXI (1929), 211, n. 8.

[19]S. R. R., XVII (1925), 227, n. 17. Cf. also S. R. R., XV (1923), 25-31, nn. 3-4.

du mariage) was considered by the Rota as insufficient of itself to indicate simulation,[20] though it is evident that in other circumstances the phrase could deserve to be otherwise interpreted. In the same way the phrase, *Mi sposo per un capriccio,* was interpreted as expressing not the intention of simulating, but rather the intention of contracting a true marriage, though without due seriousness.[21] The interpretation was given in the light of the particular circumstances of the case, it is true, yet it is significant that such phrases may be reconciled with true consent though they connote a full expression of the truth.

On the contrary, frequent repetitions of statements to the effect that the party had no desire to marry, when made before the ceremony.[22] declarations that the marriage was against one's wishes,[23] acts that were planned with a view to forestalling the ceremony,[24] and assertions that the marriage ceremony was deemed not to beget any effect, that it was held not to produce any obligation, or that it was simply regarded as a comedy,[25] exemplify more evident indications of the intention of simulating.

In every case the particular context, circumstances and personalities concerned will have to be considered.[26] A statement made under the influence of anger, for example, is frequently an inaccurate manifestation of a person's true intention.[27] Likewise a person's claim that his consent was fictitious may have been merely a jest.[28]

Finally, a party's assertions regarding his own intention may possess very slight probative value because of the un-

[20] S. R. R., XXI (1929), 214, n. 11.
[21] S. R. R., XXVII (1935), 552, n. 3.
[22] S. R. R., XXIX (1937), 100, n. 4; S. R. R., XVI (1924), 70-71, n. 4.
[23] Cf. S. R. R., XVIII (1926), 256, n. 10; S. R. R., XVII (1925), 69, n. 3; S. R. R., III (1911), 350, n. 9.
[24] S. R. R., XXIX (1937), 100, n. 4.
[25] Cf. S. R. R., XXVI (1934), 471-2, n. 8; S. R. R., XX (1928), 394-5, n. 6; S. R. R., XV (1923), 226, n. 7; S. R. R., III (1911), 18, n. 6.
[26] S. R. R., XXIX (1937), 563, n. 11.
[27] Cf. S. R. R., XXX (1938), 346-7, nn. 4-5; S. R. R., XXVIII (1936), 134, n. 7.
[28] Cf. S. R. R., XXVI (1934), 76, n. 12; S. R. R., VI (1914), 252, n. 17.

reliability and untrustworthiness of his character.[29] In these cases the proofs will have to be drawn in their entirety from the alleged cause of the simulation, and from the circumstantial evidence. These factors will be treated in the following two chapters.

---

[29]Cf. S. R. R., XXVII (1935), 552, n. 3; S. R. R., XXI (1929), 174, n. 6.

CHAPTER VII

THE CAUSE OF THE SIMULATION

The primary end of marriage is the procreation and education of children; its secondary end is mutual help and the allaying of concupiscence.[1] The word "end" *(finis)* denotes a good towards the realization of which an act tends either by its nature or by the deliberate intention of the agent. The *finis operis* of matrimony is the good towards which marriage tends by its nature. The *finis operantis* of matrimony is that good towards the realization of which the will of the contractant is directed.[2]

It is evident that a person does not necessarily commit a fault simply because his purpose in marrying is not identical with the end of marriage. As long as this purpose is morally good, or at least indifferent, the consort fulfills the law.[3] Moreover, even if the party marries for a sinful purpose, the contract is valid as long as there is no exclusion of the essence of matrimony or of its essential properties.[4]

A person who marries with a purpose in mind which is other than the purpose of marriage may do so in one of two ways. (1)

---

[1]Canon 1013, § 1.

[2]S. R. R., n. 9—*AAS*, XXXVI (1944), 184 ff.

[3]Gasparri, *De Matrimonio*, I, n. 9; Cappello, *De Sacramentis*, III, n. 12; Coronata, *De Sacramentis*, III, n. 5; Chelodi, *De Matrimonio*, n. 3; Payen, *De Matrimonio*, I, n. 82; Wernz-Vidal, *Ius Matrimoniale*, n. 26; Vermeersch-Creusen, *Epitome Iuris Canonici*, II, n. 275; De Smet, *De Sponsalibus et Matrimonio*, nn. 85-86; Bayón, *De Matrimonio*, I, n. 23; Heylen, *De Matrimonio*, p. 149; Bouscaren-Ellis, *Canon Law*, p. 400; Ayrinhac, *Marriage Legislation in the New Code of Canon Law*, n. 4.

[4]"Compertum est enim quod fines, vel honesti vel etiam indifferentes, extranei tamen in contractu matrimonii, non reddunt matrimonium ne ullo quidem modo culpabile; quodque fines, etiamsi mali, non adversantes tamen essentiae matrimonii eiusque bonis, in neutro foro irritant matrimonium, quia cum illis finibus, qui eliguntur ut rationes applicationis ad matrimonium, stat finis matrimonii debitus, etiamsi tunc non cognitatus, quia virtute intenditur in ipso contractu, cum non excluditur."—S. R. R., XXI (1929), 550, n. 8.

The extrinsic purpose may be considered as the secondary cause of the marriage. As such it is a reason for marrying, and without it the marriage would not be contracted. In this case the *finis operantis* does not exclude the *finis operis*: the purpose of attaining a particular end, even though it be the cause of the contract, does not destroy the objective end of matrimony. (2) On the other hand, the extrinsic purpose may be considered as the final and exclusive cause of the contract, whereby it alone is intended by the contractant to the exclusion of the proper end of matrimony. This is the case, for example, when a party regards and intends the celebration of matrimony as an empty ceremony and submits to it for the sole purpose of financial gain. The contractant excludes the objective end of marriage by intruding his subjective purpose. This is what takes place in a case of total simulation.[5]

The essence of total simulation is that of a lie.[6] In simulating marital consent a person signifies that he has the intention of marrying, whereas his true intention is precisely the antithesis of this, namely, the intention of not contracting marriage. Total simulation thus implies the existence of two acts of the will on the part of the simulator. In the first place, there is the intention of not marrying. Secondly there is the intention of making a false manifestation of consent. The reason for the falsity of this manifestation is the fact that it does not conform to what is in the party's mind, that is, to his knowledge of the concomitant existence of his prior intention, that of not marrying. Hence to account for a case of total simulation one must determine the causes of these two intentions, namely: the reason why the party wished not to marry, and also the reason why he submitted to the formalities of a marriage. That is why it is necessary to establish the fact that the alleged simulator enter-

---

[5]S. R. R., XVII (1925), 378, n. 8.

[6]"Simulatio proprie dicta seu formalis est mendacium per facta, quo quis per actiones externas aliud intendit significare quam habet in mente,. . . ."—Merkelbach, *Summa Theoligiae Moralis*. (3 ed., 3 vols., Parisiis; Desclée De Brouwer et Soc., 1939), II, n. 865. Simulation of marital consent is more commonly committed by means of words than through the agency of deeds.

tained an aversion towards the other party or at least towards the marriage. Otherwise the motive prompting submission to the ceremony may have been the cause of a true marriage (a *finis operantis)*. Yet if an aversion alone is proved to have existed, and there is no evidence that there was a reason for a manifestation of consent, then, since there is not in evidence any cause that induced the person to act contrary to his aversion, the marriage must be regarded as having been freely willed in spite of the aversion.[7]

The influence of an aversion and its value as an indication of simulation will be considered in the treatment of the circumstantial evidence. For the present it will be sufficient to note that the aversion must be such as to account for a positive intention of not contracting marriage if there is to be a declaration of nullity in the case. A simple lack of love for the other party does not constitute such an aversion:. . . .*non enim amor, sed consensus facit coniugium.*[8] Similarly, a mere suspicion that the other party is not an honourable person is not tantamount to a sufficient aversion.[9]

In certain cases it may happen that, even though an aversion is entertained by the alleged simulator, it is not actually directed towards the other party or towards the marriage itself, but merely towards the circumstances of the wedding. The plaintiff in one Rota case had contracted marriage in order to obtain money to pay a debt.[10] He claimed that this brought humiliation to him, since he considered himself as being sold like an animal, and that he regarded the marriage as a sacrilege. However, the fact that he had written daily love letters to the woman before marriage, and the fact that the marriage was

---

[7]Cf. S. R. R., IV (1912), 466, n. 19, wherein it is stated that the presence of an aversion toward the other party does not of itself indicate simulation, but merely that the marriage was involuntary *secundum quid.*

[8]S. R. R., XVII (1925), 58, n. 11. Cf. also, S. R. R., XXIX (1937), 75, n. 11; S. R. R., XXIX (1937), 154, n. 10; S. R. R., XXIX (1937), 315, nn. 1, 3; S. R. R., XXVIII (1936), 102, n. 3; S. R. R., XXVII (1935), 628-630, n. 22; S. R. R., XXVI (1934), 456, n. 11; S. R. R., XXV (1933), 28-9, n. 6; S. R. R., XXIII (1931), 303, n. 19.

[9]S. R. R., XXVIII (1936), 9, n. 10.

[10]S. R. R., XXV (1933), 80, n. 4.

promptly consummated, indicated that any aversion he may have felt was not directed towards her person or towards the idea of marrying her. The Rota remarked that the consummation of the marriage weakened the claim of simulation in the case, and that an aversion towards the circumstances of the marriage could well coexist with true marital consent.[11]

In the examination of the cause of the alleged simulation it is necessary that it be distinguished from a reason for contracting a valid marriage.[12] The cause must be shown to have been sufficient and proportionate, at least in the simulator's estimation, to urge him to give an apparent manifestation of marital consent in spite of his positive intention not to contract marriage.[13]

If a person marries to obtain money he contracts validly, even though his only purpose in approaching the altar is to acquire money. Yet, financial gain may also provide a motive for simulation, as in the case when the person who submits to the marriage ceremony for the sake of obtaining money has the positive intention of not marrying. Indeed, the financial gain may have been sufficient to cause the person to simulate a consent for marriage even though for one reason or another he never actually obtained the money afterwards. Thus the motive as alleged may have been sufficient to prompt the simulation in spite of the fact that the cherished purpose was not actually realized by means of the perpetrated simulation.[14]

There are certain causes to which simulation is sometimes attributed in particular cases, but which by their nature seem to indicate that a true marital consent was given rather than excluded. Such is the case when a person claims that he married solely to prevent the other party from marrying a third person,

---

[11]*Ibidem*, pp. 82-83, n. 7.

[12]S. R. R., XXIX (1937), 316, n. 4; S. R. R. XXVI (1934), 673, n. 3; S. R. R. XV (1923), 167, n. 4.

[13]"Imprimis vero constet de causa simulandi, quae prorsus distinguitur a causa matrimonii ipsius; seu demonstretur oportet adfuisse rationem ita sufficientem et proportionatam in simulantis existimatione, ut hic contrahere matrimonium positive nolens, sed nullum aliud effugium habens, impulsus fuerit ad proferendum ore quod corde non teneret."—S. R. R., XVI (1924), 313-314, n. 3. Cf., also S. R. R., XXIX (1937), 154, n. 10.

[14]Cf. S. R. R., XXIX (1937), 567, n. 19.

or in order to be able to continue carnal relations already begun, or simply to quiet the conscience of the other party.[15] The same presumption seems deducible from the motive of providing for a child already conceived,[16] of satisfying what one feels to be a moral obligation to marry the other party.[17]

Indeed the positive intention of contracting marriage to obtain a definite end clearly excludes the possibility of simulation.[18] Matrimonial consent is not ordinarily given in such a manner that it depends for its existence upon the verification of the cause which prompted the marriage.[19] The fact that a woman is disappointed after her wedding in the size of her husband's fortune is patently no indication that she simulated matrimonial consent in order to share the fortune of the other party.[20] For the same reason, namely, that marital consent does not depend for its validity upon the cause for which the marriage is entered, the intention of contracting a true marriage and the intention of defrauding one's spouse are not mutually contradictory.[21]

After it has been established that a possible cause of simulation existed in a particular instance, there remains to be proved the fact that it was sufficiently grave and proportionate to induce the individual person in the particular circumstances to simulate matrimony.[22] It is sufficient if the contractant considered the cause as grave, true and relevant, even though ob-

---

15S. R. R., VI (1914), 330, n. 12.

16Cf. S. R. R., XXX (1938), 347, n. 5; S. R. R., XXI (1929), 304, n. 6.

17Cf. S. R. R., XXVIII (1936), 102, n. 3; S. R. R., XXI (1929), 263, n. 9.

18Porro positiva in casu voluntas matrimonii contrahendi ad determinatum propositumque finem obtinendum simulationem consensus manifeste excludit."—S. R. R., XXVI (1934), 413, n. 10.

19"Nam consensus matrimonialis non datur dependenter a causa propter quam matrimonium contrahitur, sed se habet concomitanter ad illam."—Wernz, *Ius Decretalium*, (2 ed., Romae et Prati, 1906-1913), Vol. IV, n. 304.

20Cf. S. R. R., IV (1912), 406, n. 12; S. R. R., XXVI (1934), 415, n. 14.

21S. R. R., XXI (1929), 552, n. 11; S. R. R., XX (1928), 112, n. 9.

22". . . . .necesse est simulandi causam adfuisse, quae fuerit gravis, manifesta et proportionata, in simulantis quidem consideratione, cum ipse, per ritum externe impletum, omnia coniugii onera coram lege ecclesiastica et civili in se suscipere tenetur. Et distincte opus est, quod causa apta intervenerit, non ad contractum ineundum, sed ad simulationem eo in contractu inducendam."— S. R. R., XXIII (1931), 294, n. 4. Cf. also S. R. R., XXIX (1937), 103-104, n. 8; S. R. R., XXV (1933), 387, n. 4; S. R. R., XVI (1924), 70, n. 3.

jectively it was not so.[23] Consequently the character of the person accused of simulation must be made well known to the court. If the cause of the alleged simulation is an immoral one, it must be established that the party's character was such that he would be moved by such a motive. The Rota has upheld validity in several cases principally because it was considered that the person's character was not proved to have been sufficiently immoral to have warranted his acting in the manner that was alleged.[24] On the other hand, the mere fact that the party is shown to have been of unworthy character does not establish the fact that he simulated matrimonial consent, as is evident.[25]

The desire to obtain money either from the other party to the marriage or from a third person, regardless of the intensity of this desire, does not constitute in itself an evident and proportionate motive for simulation, since it does not necessarily exclude the intention of contracting a true marriage for this purpose.[26] This is especially true when the party did not manifest any aversion towards the other contractant or towards the marriage.[27] It is only when a person marries for money alone, in such a manner that he wishes the money without the other party, that he is guilty of simulation. When a man simulates consent for this purpose, it almost inevitably happens that he deserts the woman after he has received the money: once his purpose in

---

[23]Wanenmacher, "Some questions on vitiated marital consent,"—*The Ecclesiastical Review*, CI (1939), 133.

[24]Cf. S. R. R., XXIX (1937), 75, n. 11; S. R. R., XXIX (1937), 665, n. 6; S. R. R., XXIII (1931), 301, n. 16; S. R. R., XXII (1930), 376, n. 9.

[25]Cf. S. R. R., XXVI (1934), 75-76, n. 11; S. R. R., XXVI (1934), 167-8, n. 4; S. R. R., XXV (1933) 452-3, nn. 3-6; S. R. R., XXI (1929), 263, n. 9.

[26]". . . voluntas comparandi pecuniam per matrimonium non constituit de se causam manifestam proportionatamque tantae simulationis; huiusmodi appetitio utique impellere potest ad contrahendum, sed non excludit de necessitate voluntatem contrahendi pure et simpliciter matrimonium. . . ."—S. R. R., XXII (1930), 387, n. 5.

[27]". . pecuniae desiderium, quamvis vehemens, optime cum voluntate componitur contrahendi matrimonium. Desiderium enim hoc est ratio qua quis movetur ad mulierem divitem ducendam, potius quam pauperem, quae ratio nihil omnino impedit, quominus divite muliere semel electa, cum ea matrimonium cum vero consensu, prout de iure, contrahat: adeo ut lucri captandi et matrimonii contrahendi voluntas simul consistant; illa veluti causa occasionalis et etiam motiva, quae istam ad matrimonium determinat pure et simpliciter contrahendum praesertim quando, ut in casu, animi abest aversio."— S. R. R., XII (1920), 50-51, n. 6.

simulating has been realized, he has no reason to continue the hoax.[28]

In the event that the motive alleged for simulation is the satisfaction of lustful desires towards the other party, the explanation for the intention of not contracting a true marriage is to be sought, not so much in the fact of an aversion towards the other party, as towards marriage itself. To prove that such a desire was the cause of a simulation, it must be established that it could be satisfied in no other way than by pretending to marry. In cases of this nature an analysis of the character of the person accused of the simulation is of capital importance.[29]

Purposes of lust have provided motives for simulation also in another manner. Some persons, usually they are women, have given a fictitious matrimonial consent in order to escape the authority of their parents or other superiors in order that they might be free to continue their sinful manner of living with impunity.[30] The invalidity of marriages which have been contracted in such circumstances is frequently due to partial simulation or to force and fear.[31]

If it has been proved in a particular case that a party married under duress, it is not always easy for the judge to determine whether the person totally simulated consent or whether he gave a consent that was deficient because of force and fear. Provided that the fear was sufficient to nullify matrimonial consent, the invalidity of the marriage can be lawfully declared even though it cannot be determined which of the two species of deficient consent actually caused the nullity.[32]

---

[28]"Aliter vero dicendum est, si contrahens ex 'auri sacra fame' tantummodo inhiat pecuniae sponsae, quin intendat contrahere matrimonium cum puella, idest si vult pecuniam, non autem vult mulierem. Quo in casu vir, capta dote, mulierem relinquere solet Suum finem enim assecutus est atque ideo matrimonio ficte inito valedicit."—S. R. R., XXVI (1934), 72, n. 4.

[29]Cf. S. R. R., XXII (1930), 380-381, n. 14; S. R. R., XVIII (1926), 36, n. 8; S. R. R., XVIII (1926), 234, n. 5; S. R. R., XV (1923), 226, n. 7; S. R. R., III (1911), 21, n. 10.

[30]Cf. S. R. R., XXIV (1932), 76, n. 14; S. R. R., XXIII (1931), 79, n. 12; *Fontes*, n. 4211. The same cause was alleged but remained unproven in the following cases: S. R. R., XXVI (1934), 168-170, nn. 5-7; S. R. R., XXIII (1931), 297, n. 9; S. R. R., XV (1923), 168, n. 6.

[31]Cf. S. R. R., XV (1923), 168, n. 6.

[32]"Iamvero si quis probatur esse ob gravem coactionem adductum ad matrimonium, haud semper facile erit, praesertim si rudis sit in-

To render marriage invalid, the fear that influences the consort must be grave and unjustly inspired from without, in such a manner that in order to escape it the person is compelled to choose marriage.[33] However, in order to provide an adequate cause of simulation, fear need not possess all of these qualities.[34] Total simulation is caused by fear when the consort believes that he cannot escape the wedding without suffering a grave evil, and thus he indeed fulfills the external requisites of the ceremony, but consents only verbally since he has the definite and firm intention of not contracting marriage.[35]

A fear that is justly inflicted *ab intrinseco* may provide a sufficient cause of simulation.[36] Moreover, in order that the influence of fear be considered as an adequate cause of simulation in a particular case, it is not necessary that the gravity of the fear be the equivalent of that which the law demands in order that a marriage be declared null on the ground of force and

---

genii, discernere utrum, non obstante externa consensus expressione, interius consensum absolute denegaverit, an consensum aliqualem saltem dederit; at, coactione probata, ut supponitur, in utroque casu matrimonium invalidum est: aut enim nullus praestitus est verus consensus, tum deficit matrimonium; aut consensus datus est, sed ipso iure irritus est. Quapropter probatu metu sufficienti ad matrimonium invalidandum, invaliditas matrimonii declarari legitime potest, etsi haud aperte decerni possit, consensus simulatusne fuerit, an revera datus, sed ob metum irritus."—S. R. R., XIX (1927), 316, n. 3. Cf. also S. R. R., XIX (1927), 466-472; S. R. R., XVII (1925), 68, n. 2.

[33]Canon 1087, § 1: "Invalide quoque est matrimonium initum ob vim vel metum gravem ab extrinseco et iniuste incussum, a quo ut quis se liberet, eligere cogatur matrimonium.

§ 2. Nullus alius metus, etiamsi det causam contractui, matrimonii nullitatem secumfert."

[34]"Etsi non agatur de metu ex sese dirimente matrimonium, quoniam scilicet deest saltem una ex notis necessario requisitis ad reddendum matrimonium nullum, eiusmodi metus apta potest esse simulationis causa."—S. R. R., XXIII (1931), 226, n. 5.

[35]"Metus agit ut causa simulationis, si nupturiens metu impellitur ad simulandum consensum, quia existimans se absque gravi malo non posse evitare odiosam celebrationem, ritum quidem perficit, sed solum labiis, seu verba consensus profert cum certa ac firma voluntate aut non contrahendi aut reiiciendi unum saltem ex bonis substantialibus matrimonii."—S. R. R., XXIII (1931), 124, n. 2.

[36]S. R. R., XXVI (1934), 735, n. 14.

fear.[37] Yet a light fear would not supply a sufficient cause of simulation.[38]

In one case brought before the Rota, the woman claimed that she had married a man who was displeasing to her, simply for the reason that the marriage was desired by her foster-parents, who had been very kind to her. At most, this fear would have been but very light. However, the Rota considered the woman's motive to have been more akin to gratitude.[39] Gratitude, however, can be a reason for giving a true consent to marriage, and hence does not necessarily indicate simulation.[40]

Finally, though a light fear does not suffice as a cause for total simulation, it is not necessary that the fear or the cause of the simulation be actually true, or relevant, or operative; it is sufficient that it be held to be such in the mind of the simulator.[41]

The various purposes that may motivate a person in the perpetration of a total simulation may be classified under one or the other of the following types: a party simulates marital consent in order to obtain something that he desires, or in order to avoid something that seems to him to be an evil. Examples of the first type that have been considered are financial gain and the satisfaction of lust: in connection with the avoidance of or escape from an evil the influence of fear has been mentioned. These are the principal causes of total simulation in the cases that have been decided by the Rota. An appreciation of the particular forms in which these motives may appear can be obtained only from an analysis of the cases in which they existed. The following table is offered as an aid in the accomplishment of this task.

---

[37] "Ut quis dicatur metu inductum fuisse ad simulandum, sane non requiritur gravitas illa metus qualem iura requirunt ut matrimonium ex capite metus nullum declaretur."—S. R. R., XVI (1924), 318, n. 7. Cf. S. R. R., XXVI (1934), 728, n. 2; S R. R., V (1913), 212, n. 6.

[38] S. R. R., XXVI (1934), 729, n. 3.

[39] S. R. R., XVII (1925), 177-8, n. 7.

[40] S. R. R., XVII (1925), 377, n. 7.

[41] S. R. R., XVI (1924), 69, n. 3: ". . .necesse non est ut metus seu causa simulandi sit verus, relevans et subsistens, sed sufficit quod sit a simulante opinatus." Cf. S. R. R., III (1911), 241, n. 9.

Rota Cases of Total Simulation Arranged According to Alleged Causes of the Simluation

CAUSE ALLEGED	CONSTAT	NON-CONSTAT
Financial Gain.	S. R. R., XXX (1938), 587, n. 4. S. R. R., XXVI (1934), 467, nn. 4-5. S. R. R., XXIV (1932), 76, n. 14. S. R. R., VII (1915), 197-8, nn. 5-6. S. R. R., III (1911), 20-21, nn. 9-10. S. R. R., III (1911), 326, n. 3.	S. R. R., XXVI (1934), 74, n. 8. S. R. R., XXVI (1934), 456, n. 11. S. R. R., XXVI (1934), 676, n. 9. S. R. R., XXV (1933), 80, n. 4. S. R. R., XXV (1933), 452-3, nn. 3-6. S. R. R., XXI (1929), 550, n. 8. S. R. R., XX (1928), 247, n. 3. S. R. R., XX (1928), 112, n. 9. S. R. R., XIX (1927), 197, n. 5. S. R. R., XVII (1925), 377, n. 8. S. R. R., XV (1923), 25, n., 3. S. R. R., XII (1920), 50, n. 6. S. R. R., VI (1914), 246, n. 6.
Temporal advantage to or to please a third party.	S. R. R., XXVI (1934), 467, nn. 4-5.	S. R. R., XXVIII (1936), 110, n. 13. S. R. R., XXVIII (1936), 130, n. 3. S. R. R., XXVI (1934), 170, nn. 7-9. S. R. R., XXI (1929), 550, n. 8. S. R. R., XX (1928), 247, n. 3. S. R. R., XV (1923), 144, n. 7. S. R. R., IV (1912), 462, n. 8.
Sexual gratification.	S. R. R., XXIII (1931), 287, n. 4. S. R. R., XXI (1929), 234, n. 5. S. R. R., XVIII (1926), 36, n. 8. S. R. R., III (1911), 20-21, nn. 9-10.	
To continue immoral life.	S. R. R., XXIV (1932), 76, n. 14. S. R. R., XXIII (1912), 79, n. 12.	S. R. R., XXVI (1934), 169, n. 6. S. R. R., XXIII (1931), 297, n. 9. S. R. R., XV (1923), 168, n. 6.
Desire for civil effects of marriage.	S. R. R., XVI (1924), 155, n. 5.	S. R. R., XXVI (1934), 413, n. 10. S. R. R., XXIII (1931), 142, n. 11. S. R. R., XXII (1930), 469-472, nn. 19-22. S. R. R., XXI (1929), 304, n. 6. S. R. R., XVI (1924), 155, n. 9. S. R. R., VIII (1916), 54, n. 10.

CAUSE ALLEGED	CONSTAT	NON-CONSTAT
Fear Arising from pregnancy, intercourse or seduction.	S. R. R., XX (1928), 394, n. 5.	S. R. R., XXX (1938), 347, n. 5.
	S. R. R., XXVI (1924), 155, n. 5.	S. R. R., XXX (1938), 642, n. 5.
	S. R. R., XII (1920), 70, n. 11.	S. R. R., XXIX (1937), 739, n. 10.
	S. R. R., XI (1919), 38, n. 5.	S. R. R., XXVI (1934), 413, n. 10.
	S. R. R., III (1911), 241, n. 10.	S. R. R., XXV (1933), 393, n. 18.
		S. R. R., XXV (1933), 446, n. 7.
		S. R. R., XXV (1933), 465, n. 7.
		S. R. R., XXV (1933), 573, n. 10.
		S. R. R., XXIII (1931), 229, n. 10.
		S. R. R., XXII (1930), 469, n. 19.
		S. R. R., XXI (1929), 264, n. 10.
		S. R. R., XXI (1929), 304, n. 6.
		S. R. R., XIX (1927), 173, n. 7.
Threat of jail sentence.	S. R. R., XXVI (1934), 9, n. 11.	S. R. R., XXIX (1937), 71, n. 3.
	S. R. R., III (1911), 241, n. 10.	S. R. R., XXVI (1934), 730, n. 4.
		S. R. R., XXIII (1931), 229, n. 10.
		S. R. R., XXI (1929), 550, n. 8.
		S. R. R., XIX (1927), 173, n. 7.
To avoid scandal or loss of reputation.	S. R. R., XVIII (1926), 256, n. 9.	S. R. R., XXIX (1937), 75, n. 11,
	S. R. R., XI (1919), 38, n. 5.	S. R. R., XXIX (1937), 739, n. 10.
	S. R. R., III (1911), 241, n. 10.	S. R. R., XXVI (1934), 413, n. 10.
		S. R. R., XXVI (1934), 730, n. 4.
		S. R. R., XXV (1933), 393, n. 18.
		S. R. R., XIX (1927), 190, n. 16.
		S. R. R., XVI (1924), 314, n. 4.
Other cases of fear.	S. R. R., XXIX (1937), 101, n. 5.	S. R. R., XXIX (1937), 152, n. 7.
	S. R. R., XX (1928), 345, n. 6.	S. R. R., XXIX (1937), 533, n. 12.
	S. R. R., XIX (1927), 216, n. 4.	S. R. R., XXVII (1935), 624, n. 10.
	S. R. R., XVI (1924), 69, n. 3.	S. R. R., XXV (1933), 243, n. 3.
	S. R. R., V (1913), 212, n. 6.	S. R. R., XXIV (1932), 152 ff.
		S. R. R., XXIII (1931), 66, n. 15.
		S. R. R., XXIII (1931), 198, n. 9.
		S. R. R., XXI (1929), 513, n. 8.
		S. R. R., XVIII (1926), 255, n. 8.
		S. R. R., XVII (1925), 54, n. 8.
		S. R. R., XVII (1925), 177. n. 7.
		S. R. R., VIII (1916), 199, n. 4.
		S. R. R., IV (1912), 406, n. 12.

CHAPTER VIII

CIRCUMSTANTIAL EVIDENCE

The circumstances of a particular case comprise indications of simulation when certain and determined facts which are mutually confirmatory are so connected with the alleged simulation that moral certitude of the fictitious consent may be had.[1] It is left to the judge to estimate what conjectures suffice for the begetting of moral certitude in each case,[2] though it is apparent that greater force is to be attributed to indications according as their proximity to the act is greater.[3]

A legitimate presumption in favor of the existence of simulation in a particular case is usually based on more than one of the facts that have been established as evidence. Since the circumstances and their juxtaposition are different in each case, it would be rash to attribute in all cases a similar probative value to the presence of a particular circumstance. Indeed, the Rota itself warns against such unwarranted generalization.[4] This admonition is to be borne in mind in the following treatment of circumstantial evidence. It must also be remembered that for an accurate evaluation of the circumstances connected with former cases a consultation of the actual decisions is required.

1S. R. R., XXVI (1934), 637, n. 4.

2S. R. R., XXVII (1935), 79-80, n. 6. Cf. Sanchez, *De Matrimonio*, Lib. II, Disp. XLV, n. 5; Laymann, *Theologia Moralis* Lib. V, Tract. X, Par. II, Cap. VI, n. 2.

3S. R. R., XV, (1923), 167, n. 5.

4S. R. R., I (1909), 59, n. 13: ". . . . .resolutiones S. Congregationis non facile esse trahendas de casu ad casum, . . ." The reference is to the Sacred Congregation of the Council, which handled matrimonial cases prior to the reestablishment of the Rota in 1909.

Article I

The Circumstances Antecedent to the Ceremony

Simulated matrimonial consent can be explained only in the light of the simulator's repugnance for the other party or at least for the idea of marrying this party.[5] The establishment of the fact that the parties were happy in their engagement or that there was a mutual affection between them would be detrimental to the cause of the plaintiff. The fact of a friendship and affection before marriage usually outweighs the claim that the ceremony was submitted to only because of parental urgings, the fear of scandal, the loss of reputation, etc.[6] The usual tokens such as love-letters and frequent visits serve to establish the existence of such a friendship.[7]

Similarly, when the party has declared before the ceremony that he desired to marry, there is an indication that his marital consent was not feigned.[8] The fact of pre-marital carnal relations between the parties, when accompanied with mutual affection, may provide a grave indication of genuine consent.[9] However, the same force would not attach to this fact if it were established that the parties' feelings for each other had changed before the ceremony, though quarrels over minor issues would not suffice to indicate such a change.[10] The simulator's manifestation of affection for the other party is evidently of less value as an indication of true

---

[5] S. R. R., XXV (1933), 82, n. 7: "In qua inquisitione fundamentum profecto praebere debet certo demonstrata aversio et repugnantia contrahentis a persona cum qua matrimonium init."

[6] Cf. X. R. R., XXX (1938), 346, n. 5; S. R. R., XXIX (1937), 670, n. 13; S. R. R., XXVIII (1936), 11, n. 3; S. R. R., XXIII (1931), 197-8, nn. 8-9; S. R. R., XXI (1929), 209, n. 5; S. R. R., XXI (1929), 551-2, n. 10; S. R. R., XX (1928), 246, n. 3; S. R. R., XIX (1927), 174, n. 8.

[7] Cf. S. R. R., XXV (1933), 80, n. 4; S. R. R., XXV (1933), 246, n. 10; S. R. R., XXII (1930), 387-8, nn. 5-6; S. R. R., XVI (1924), 316, n. 5; S. R. R., XII (1920), 50, n. 6; S. R. R., VI (1914), 247, n. 7; S. R. R., II (1910), 329, n. 16; S. R. R., XXIII (1931), 198, n. 9.

[8] Cf. X. R. R., XXIX (1937), 739, n. 12; S. R. R., XXVIII (1936), 99-100, n. 1; S. R. R., XXI (1929), 551-2, n. 10.

[9] Cf. S. R. R., XXX (1938), 346-7, n. 5; S. R. R., XXI (1929), 263, n. 9; S. R. R., XXI (1929), 551-2, n. 10; S. R. R., XV (1923), 36, n. 8.

[10] Cf. S. R. R., XIX (1927), 190, n. 16.

consent in the case wherein the purpose of the deception was the satisfaction of his lustful desires.

On the other hand, the fact that a party was depressed or unhappy during the engagement does not of itself indicate that his consent to marriage was fictitious.[11] Yet, when the despondency was accompanied with a reluctance to express consent to the marriage, and with confirmatory circumstances after the marriage, it may be sufficient to render the judge morally certain that the consent was not genuine, provided that a sufficient cause for the simulation has been established.[12] A fear or reluctance to enter the married state, if unaccompanied with other circumstances, indicates the intention of giving a true consent rather than a simulated one.[13]

The desire "to get the marriage over with" as soon as possible is not incompatible with true consent,[14] though it may provide subsidiary evidence when the simulation was motivated by the desire for money, of carnal relations, or of freedom from parental authority.[15] Similarly, efforts made to postpone the ceremony may be explained by motives of expediency, such as the fear of arousing parental wrath, and do not necessarily imply the intention of not marrying.[16] Efforts or the desire to avoid the wedding entirely provide graver indications of an aversion, especially when fear has been established as a cause for simulation.[17] Yet it would still be necessary to show that there had been no change of heart before the ceremony.[18]

Coolness towards the other party may be indicative of the absence of infatuation, or of the presence of some external in-

---

11S. R. R., XXVIII (1936), 317, n. 18; S. R. R., XXIII (1931), 298, n. 11.

12Cf. S. R. R., V (1913), 286, n. 5.

13S. R. R., XIII (1931), 276, n. 6: ". . . .ipse timor martimonii ineundi, vel initi dolor, conscientiam arguit contrahendi vel contracti vinculi per consensum praestandum vel praestitum, potius quam simulandi intentionem."

14S. R. R., XXIII (1931), 298, n. 10.

15Cf. S. R. R., XXIII (1931), 81, n. 13.

16S. R. R., XXV (1933), 444-447, nn. 4-9; S. R. R., XXV (1933), 395, n. 21

17S. R. R., XXIX (1937), 100-101, n. 4; S. R. R., XVIII (1926), 256, n. 8.

18Cf. S. R. R., XV (1923), 25-27, n. 3; S. R. R., XXV (1933), 216, n. 10.

fluence, but it alone cannot form the basis for a presumption of simulation.[19] It would offer supporting evidence when a cause for simulation has been established and the person's opposition to the marriage has been brought to light from the other facts of the case.[20]

An indication of spurious consent is had when it is shown that until the moment of the marriage, the party continually expressed his desire to marry someone else.[21] It is presupposed that in this case an adequate reason for the simulation has been verified. A common indication of such an attachment is in evidence when a person is shown to have had continual sexual relations with the third party until the time of the wedding.[22] It is evident that the fact of such relations does not render the subsequent marital consent presumptively invalid, and in several instances the Rota has disregarded it as insufficient evidence, especially when no adequate cause for the simulation had been established.[23] The same fact, however, may be of great value when the motive alleged for the simulation is the escape from parental authority in order to continue an immoral life,[24] or simply the satisfaction of sinful desires toward the other party.[25]

The fact that a lengthy period of betrothal has preceded a marriage lessens the possibility that a lack of affection would remain unperceived by the other consort. For this reason the

---

[19] S. R. R., XXVIII (1936), 615, n. 18; S. R. R., VIII (1916), 200, n. 7; S. R. R., XVI (1924), 316, n. 6.

[20] Cf. S. R. R., III (1911), 350, n. 9.

[21] S. R. R., XXI (1929), 238, n. 15; S. R. R., V (1913), 213 n. 7; S. R. R., XVII (1925), 69, n. 3.

[22] S. R. R., XXVII (1935), 526, n. 12; S. R. R., XXVI (1934), 470, n. 6; S. R. R., XVII (1925), 108-109, n. 1; S. R. R., XV (1923), 170, n. 9; S. R. R., XIV (1922), 310, n. 6; S. R. R., VII (1915), 201, n. 9; S. R. R., III (1911), 19 n. 8; S. R. R., III (1911), 347, n. 3; *Fontes*, n. 4259.

[23] "Quoad autem cum aliis viris amores, quibus conventa dicitur ante nuptias indulsisse, per se non inducunt praecisam de simulatione coniecturam, nisi forte peculiares circumstantiae accedant."—S. R. R., XXIII (1931), 303, n. 19. Cf. also S. R. R., XXIX (1937), 669, n. 13; S. R. R., XXVII (1935), 554-5, n. 6; S. R. R., XXV (1933), 450-3, nn. 1-8; S. R. R., XX (1928), 246, n. 3.

[24] S. R. R., XXIII (1931), 81, n. 13.

[25] Cf. S. R. R., III (1911), 19, n. 8.

claim that such an indifference existed may well be called into doubt in certain cases.[26]

When it has been alleged that a marriage was simulated for the purpose of financial gain, there are certain circumstances which, if verified in the particular case, seem to contradict such a claim, namely, the fact that the person accused of simulation cherished an affection towards the other party,[27] that he desired the marriage even before he fell into financial straits,[28] that he postponed the wedding or attempted to postpone it,[29] or that he had previously refused a richer person as spouse.[30]

The same presumption in favor of the giving of a true consent would hold if the person who is accused of simulation had not been in need of money, or if he had gone to considerable expense to prepare a home, to please his bride, etc.[31] Indications supporting the contention that simulation took place for financial profit are usually to be sought in the character of the person accused, in the deception of the other consort,[32] and in his preparations to desert the other party when the money had been obtained.[33]

When a man has simulated consent in order to possess the woman carnally, the circumstances of the case will usually reveal that he had previously attempted to seduce her but was unsuccessful in the attempt,[34] and that his deception of the woman regarding his intention was accompanied with other falsehoods.[35]

When pregnancy has occurred before marriage, so that there arose the question of the preserving of a reputation, the presumption seems to be in favor of the giving of a genuine marital consent rather than of one that was simulated. This is especially so when it is evident that the man intended to repair the harm

---

26Cf. S. R. R., XXIX (1937), 670, n. 13; S. R. R., XXVIII (1936), 133, n. 6; S. R. R., VI (1914), 247, n. 7.

27S. R. R., XXV (1933), 282-3, n. 7; S. R. R., XXI (1929), 551-2, n. 10.

28S. R. R., XII (1920). 50, n. 6.

29S. R. R., XXV (1933), 453-4, n. 8; S. R. R., XVII (1925), 375, n. 4.

30S. R. R., XVII (1925), 375, n. 4.

31S. R. R., XVII (1925), 375, n. 4.

32S. R. R., VII (1915), 198-200, nn. 6-8.

33S. R. R., III (1911), 329, n. 6.

34Cf. S. R. R., XVIII (1926), 37, n. 9.

35Cf. S. R. R., XXI (1929), 237-8, n. 12.

done to the woman.[36] If the man's affection for the woman had ceased and he had married under duress, there would be no basis for a presumption of this nature.[37]

If a parent's opposition to the wedding is the only motive that could explain a simulation, the claim that a fictitious consent was given to the marriage must be considered as unproved. Such opposition could explain a refusal to marry, but not a simulation.[38] However, in a case of duress when it has been proved that a party to a marriage viewed it with contempt, horror, aversion, and unwillingness, there is a strong foundation for a presumption that the consent was not genuine.[39] If the party had expressed a like hatred towards divorce, at some time previous to the marriage, there would be a basis for a presumption that the consent was a true one.[40]

The presumption of canon 1086, § 1, obtains also in those cases wherein a party knows or believes that the marriage is invalid because of a diriment of divine or ecclesiastical law.[41] Nevertheless, when it has been established that a consort believed the marriage he was contracting to be null because of the existence of such an impediment, there may arise a suspicion that he did not intend a true marriage, even though true marital consent is compatible with this erroneous belief.[42] One who knows or thinks that the marriage which he is entering cannot be valid is more easily led by this knowledge or opinion to simulate matrimony. Certainly, if the party intends the union merely as concubinage with a civil rite, the marriage is null, though more likely on the ground of partial simulation than of total.[43]

In 1929 the Rota declared the nullity of a marriage that had been contracted in the following circumstances. The previous marriage of a certain formal heretic (the defendant in the present case) had been contracted invalidly because

---

[36]S. R. R., XXIII (1931), 232, n. 18.
[37]Cf. S. R. R., XVII (1925), 69, n. 3; S. R. R., XII (1920), 63-4, n. 1.
[38]S. R. R., XXIII (1931), 232, n. 18.
[39]Wanenmacher, *Canonical Evidence in Marriage Cases*, n. 451.
[40]S. R. R., XXX (1938), 347, n. 5.
[41]Gasparri, *De Matrimonio*, nn. 812-813.
[42]Canon 1085; Gasparri, *loc. cit.*
[43]Cf. S. R. R., XVII (1925), 294, n. 2.

of the lack of the Catholic form, but the nullity remained unknown to him and he considered the woman as his true spouse. Being unable to return to his putative wife because of military orders, he had subsequently become intimate with the plaintiff, and at the instance of the latter's mother had contracted matrimony with her, making no mention of his previous marriage. It was established during the proceedings that he had kept in touch with his first wife, whom he loved, until the very moment of this ceremony.[44]

These circumstances, along with the fact that he had deceived the plaintiff and her family regarding his status, falsely alleging that he was wealthy and of noble lineage, that he had employed a pseudonym in all his relations with them, and that he denied ever having considered his second marriage a true one, indicated that the whole affair was a deception perpetrated by him for the gratification of his lust.[45]

In all cases of this nature the circumstances must be carefully scrutinized, for though the concealing of a putative impediment indicates deception, the intention of the deceiver may yet be compatible with true consent.[46]

Article II

The Circumstances Concomitant with the Celebration of the Marriage

The possibility of simulation in a particular case presupposes the fact that there has been an apparent manifestation of marital consent. If the party gave a clear negative response to the pastor's interrogation, there can be no question of his having simulated consent.[47] Nor can the presumption of canon 1086, § 1, be invoked in the case

---

[44] S. R. R., XXI (1929), 234, nn. 5-7.

[45] *Ibidem*, pp. 237-238, n. 12.

[46] Cf. S. R. R., XX (1928), 106-112; S. R. R., XIX (1927), 192-198; S. R. R., XVII (1925), 293-295; Doheny, Canonical Procedure, I, 562-564; Bouscaren, *The Canon Law Digest*, II, 302.

[47] S. R. R., XXIV (1932), 153, n. 2.

wherein a party remains silent instead of expressing consent to the marriage.[48]

The person who claims to have simulated consent admits by that claim that he has given at least an external and apparent manifestation of consent. Therefore in many cases of simulation the circumstances concomitant with the ceremony are of less probative value in instances of simulation than in those of force and fear, or of the simple absence of consent, except when the simulation was caused by fear.

A matrimonial consent that is manifested by means of signs other than words effects a valid marriage. Consequently when a person gives clear signs of consent in the presence of the pastor and the witnesses, but only mumbles his refusal to consent, in such a manner that it is not perceived by those present, he would, in effect, be simulating. [49] When established as facts by the testimony of witnesses, such circumstances may constitute adminicular proof that consent was simulated.[50]

Hesitation and reluctance in consenting, or the shedding of tears in doing so, most frequently indicate a genuine rather than a fictitious consent.[51] This behavior may be explained in certain cases by the natural hesitancy or timidity of the party, by the gravity of the moment, by fear of a parent's displeasure, or by many other reasons.[52] Yet these same facts may also point to the presence of fear when it has been alleged as the cause of simulation.[53]

---

[48]Chelodi, *De Matrimonio*, n. 121.

[49]"Sed cum consensus manifestatio valeat non tantum verbis, sed etiam signis, qui indubiis signis consensum coram parocho testibusque manifestat, incertoque vocis sonu decepturus secum submisse murmurat, is procul dubio simulationis est arguendus."—S. R. R., XXIV (1932), 153, n. 2.

[50]Cf. S. R. R., XXIX (1937), 531, n. 7; S. R. R., XXIV (1932), 152-157; S. R. R., XXI (1929), 173-5, nn. 4-9.

[51]S. R. R., XXVIII (1936), 134, n. 8; S. R. R., XXVI (1934), 171, n. 10; S. R. R., XXV (1933), 454, nn. 9-10.

[52]Cf. S. R. R., XXIX (1937), 318, n. 6; S. R. R., XXIX (1937), 736, n. 5; S. R. R., XXVI (1934), 171, n. 10; S. R. R., XXV (1933), 248, n. 13; S. R. R., XXIII (1931), 233, n. 18.

[53]Cf. S. R. R., XX (1928), 345, n. 7; S. R. R., XVIII (1926), 260, n. 14; S. R. R., V (1913), 286, n. 5; S. R. R., III (1911), 350, n. 10.

In the same way, sadness on the part of one of the parties, or an indifference or coolness toward the other party, may be reconciled with true consent.[54] In other cases they may support contention that the consent was merely external.[55] On the contrary, a party's manifestation of joy and happiness on the wedding day usually provides an excellent indication of the absence of fear or aversion.[56] However, conjectures as to a person's intention are rather unreliable when they are based upon facial expressions only, especially at such solemn moments of life as is the time of marriage.[57]

The choice of a distant place or of an extraordinary hour for the wedding indicates only the desire to conceal the fact of the marriage from others, and not necessarily a simulation of marriage.[58] In this connection one should recall that persons who have been guilty of seduction ordinarily wish to conceal their crime.[59]

Finally, it should be noted that although the priest who officiated at the marriage is a *testis qualificatus* only to the fact that there was an apparent manifestation of consent, nevertheless his testimony regarding the circumstances concomitant with the ceremony may be of greater value than that of the other witnesses, and thus is to be obtained whenever possible.[60]

Article III

The Circumstances Subsequent to the Ceremony

To determine the nature of a party's intention at the moment of contracting marriage a careful examination of his mode

[54] Cf. S. R. R., XXIX (1937), 666, n. 6; S. R. R., XXV (1933), 574, n. 11; S. R. R., XIX (1927), 189, n. 13; S. R. R., XV (1923), 26, n. 3; S. R. R., XII (1920), 51, n. 7.

[55] Cf. S. R. R., XVII (1925), 72, n. 6; S. R. R., XI (1919), 43, n. 10; S. R. R., VII (1915), 201, n. 9; S. R. R., V (1913), 215, n. 10; S. R. R., III (1911), 329-330, n. 7.

[56] S. R. R., XXVIII (1936), 11, n. 13.

[57] S. R. R., XXIX (1937), 533, n. 12.

[58] Cf. S. R. R., XII (1920), 67, n. 8.

[59] S. R. R., XXIII (1931), 231, n. 18.

[60] Cf. S. R. R., XXVI (1934), 77, n. 15.

of behavior immediately after the ceremony is essential.[61] The intention of not contracting a true marriage presupposes a repugnance either towards the other contractant or towards the idea of binding oneself to that person in matrimony. Save in the case wherein the simulation was motivated by lust, any display of affection for the other consort at the beginning of conjugal life supplies a basis for a presumption that the marital consent was not merely fictitious.[62]

The natural and principal means of manifesting such an affection is the act of carnal relations. Thus the consummation of the marriage, above all when it has been prompt and frequent, furnishes a weighty indication in favor of the giving of a genuine marital consent.[63] Especially does it support the presumption that fear was not a reason for simulating consent in the particular case.[64] Although in most circumstances carnal intercourse constitutes an expression of affection, nevertheless, objectively considered, it is an act of passion, and not necessarily a manifestation of marital love.[65] Consequently the fact of sexual relations is not an inevitable indication that one party felt no aversion or repugnance for the other. In spite of the fact that a party was absolutely opposed to the marriage he may have yielded to the proximate occasion of sin provided by the circumstances after the wedding.[66]

61S. R. R., XXVI (1934), 737, n. 18.

62Cf. S. R. R., XXX (1938), 587-8, n. 4; S. R. R., XXVIII (1936), 11-12, n. 13; S R. R., XXV (1933), 249, n. 14; S. R. R., XXV (1933), 396-7, nn. 23-25; S. R. R., XXI (1929), 210, n. 6; S. R. R., XXI (1929), 264, n. 10; S. R. R., XXI (1929), 551-2, n. 10; S. R. R., XIX (1927), 174-5, n. 9; S. R. R., XVII (1925), 381-2, n. 13.

63Cf. S. R. R., XXX (1938), 348, n. 8; S. R. R., XXX (1938), 641, n. 4; S. R. R., XXVIII (1936), 11-12, n. 13; S. R. R., XXV (1933), 396, n. 23; S. R R., XXV (1933), 447, n. 10; S. R. R., XXV (1933), 574-5, n. 11; S. R. R., XXIV (1932), 83, n. 7; S. R. R., XXIII (1931), 234, n. 20; S. R. R., XXII (1930), 391, n. 12; S. R. R., XXII (1930), 474-5, n. 28; S. R. R., XXI (1929), 305, n. 7; S. R. R. XX (1928), 449, nn. 11-12; S. R. R., XVII (1925), 227, n. 9; S. R. R., VIII (1916), 198, n. 3; S. R. R., IV (1912), 405, n. 9; S. R. R., II (1910), 327 n. 16.

64Cf. S. R. R., XXVI (1934), 415, n. 13; S. R. R., XXII (1930), 201, n. 20.

65S. R. R., XIV (1922), 63, n. 10.

66Cf. S. R. R., XIX (1927), 220, n. 10; S. R. R., XII (1920), 70, n. 12; *Fontes*, 4259.

However, if the consummation of a particular marriage is to be attributed to this cause, it is necessary that the reason for not contracting a true marriage be well established from the other facts of the case. A person who is deceitful enough to simulate matrimony in order to obtain money from the other party would usually not be above inflicting this additional grave injustice.[67] When consummation has not taken place immediately or with normal frequency, there may be a basis for the presumption that intercourse was simply the effect of temptation.[68] Yet the mere fact that the consummation of the marriage was delayed does not supply apodictic proof that the marital consent was spurious, as is evident. Such a delay may possibly be explained through a number of other reasons.[69]

In a case wherein fear has prompted a woman to simulate consent, the consummation may actually have taken place against her will, and thus would not provide a basis for a presumption in favor of genuine consent.[70] To substantiate this claim it seems imperative that there be some explanation why the woman did not take refuge in flight. This would be established if the mere celebration of the marriage did not remove the cause of the simulation. Such would be the case if the woman was prevented from fleeing by the same fear that compelled her to submit to the ceremony.[71]

The fact that the marriage was never consummated at any time may well indicate that the consent of one party was feigned, especially when fear is the cause alleged for the simulation.[72] The indication would be graver if fornication had occurred between

---

[67]Cf. S. R. R., III (1911), 24-6, nn. 15-16; S. R. R., III (1911), 330, n. 8; S R. R., III (1911), 471, n. 2.

[68]Cf. S. R. R., XVIII (1926) 260, n. 15.

[69]Cf. S. R. R., XXIII (1931), 304, n. 20; S. R. R., XVI (1924), 321-2, n. 10.

[70]Cf. S. R. R., XX (1928), 346, n. 7; S. R. R., IV (1912), 376, n. 1.

[71]Cf. S. R. R., V (1913), 215, n. 11.

[72]Cf. S. R. R., XX (1928), 396-7, n. 11; S. R. R., XVII (1925), 73, n. 7; S. R. R., XVII (1925), 112, n. 6; S. R. R., XVI (1924), 72, n. 6; S. R. R., XVI (1924), 159, n. 10; S. R. R., XV (1923), 166, n. 1, (nullity declared because of the exclusion of the blessing of offspring); S. R. R., V (1913), 290, n. 14; S. R. R., III (1911), 243, n. 12; S. R. R., III (1911), 350-1, nn. 10-11; *Fontes*, 3282; 3363; 4211.
50-51, n. 6.

the parties previous to the marriage.[73] Nevertheless, in certain cases non-consummation may be the effect of other causes, such as the necessity of an immediate journey, or the sudden illness of a party, and thus would be valueless as an indication of simulated consent.[74] Moreover, the proof of the fact of non-consummation in any case is of little value unless the existence of an adequate cause of the simulation has already been well established.[75]

When one of the consorts has deserted the other immediately or almost immediately after the ceremony, there is a grave indication that his consent to the marriage was merely fictitious.[76] The mere separation of the spouses in consequence whereof cohabitation was not instituted does not imply that one consort fled the other.[77] Furthermore, flight from and desertion of the other party after a few months of cohabitation even more evidently is not the immediate flight referred to by the authors.[78]

Cohabitation pertains to the integrity and not to the essence of marriage.[79] The right to mutual help *(mutuum adiutorium)*, which includes the right to cohabitation, arises as a natural consequence of the reception of the essential marital right. Just as the primary object of the contract is not the act of generation, but the *right* to this act, so also the secondary object is not the *mutuum adiutorium,* but the right to this, and hence it includes not the fact of cohabitation but the right to it. This secondary

---

[73] S. R. R., III (1911), 243, n. 12.

[74] Cf. S. R. R., XIX (1927), 175, n. 10.

[75] Cf. S. R. R., XVI (1924), 314, n. 4; *ibidem*, pp. 321-2, n. 10; *Fontes*, 3344.

[76] "Hinc valde ad simulationis factum constabiliendum conducit fuga, quam vix initis nuptiis simulator arripuerit, seu quod alterum coniugem illico deseruerit."—S. R. R., XXV (1933), 465, n. 6. Cf. also: S. R. R., XVII (1925), 49, n. 2; S. R. R., XVII (1925), 73, n. 7; S. R. R., XVI (1924), 314 n. 3; S. R. R., XIV (1922), 311, n. 7; S. R. R., XII (1920), 70, n. 11; S. R. R., III (1911), 242-3, nn. 11-12; S. R. R., III (1911), 351, n. 11; Sanchez, *De Matrimonio*, Lib. II, Disp. XLV, n. 6; Gasparri, *De Matrimonio*, II, n. 819.

[77] "Enimvero si post actum celebrationis coniuges in diversas partes abierunt, hic discessus ex parte viri minime haberi potest ut fuga, quae foret grave simulationis indicium."—S. R. R., XXI (1929), 305, n. 7.

[78] S. R. R., VIII (1916), 57-8, n. 16.

[79] Wernz-Vidal, *Ius Matrimoniale*, n. 600.

right is neither a constitutive part, nor a necessary condition, for the existence of the primary right. Thus a marriage may be validly contracted even though the right to cohabitation is explicitly excluded.[80]

Nevertheless, when it has been established that at the time of the marriage one of the contractants had the intention of not granting to the other party the right to communal life and to the other mutual aids, this may provide an indication that he excluded the principal right of marriage (partial simulation), or even that he had the intention of not contracting a true marriage (total simulation).[81] Although this indication is insufficient to produce moral certitude of the fact of simulation, nevertheless, when there was no other cause to account for the fact that the spouses did not institute cohabitation, the assertion that the marital consent was not a true one must be considered as established, when other circumstances supply sufficient adminicular evidence.[82]

As examples of extrinsic reasons for not instituting cohabitation immediately, the following may be cited: the fact that the man has not yet procured a home to which he can bring his bride,[83] the illness of one of the parties, the necessity of departing on an immediate voyage without the other party,[84] the ne-

---

[80]S. R. R., nn. 22, 24—*AAS* XXXVI (1944), 188 ff.

[81]*Ibidem*, p. 190.

[82]"Cum igitur nulla ratione suberat, cur coniuges vitam communem non instituerent ac more aliorum coniugum se gererent, assertus defectus matrimonialis consensus. . . ., sufficienter probatus, cum ceteris adminiculis, dici debet. "—S. R. R., XVI (1924), 160, n. 10. Cf. also S. R. R., XXIII (1931), 380, n. 2; "Inter facta vero, quae consensus exclusionem expressius produnt, censendum est firmum propositum numquam instituendi vitam communem cum alttero coniuge; quamquam enim vita communis per se non pertinet ad obiectum essentiale contractus matrimonialis, practice tamen ita pertinet ad eius implementum, ut vix invenias hominem, qui, dum matrimonium serio contrahit, vitam communem deliberato excludat. "Declarations of nullity which were based on this norm are illustrated in the following cases: S. R. R., XXIX (1937), 107, n. 13; S. R. R., XXVI (1934), 9, n. 11; S. R. R., XVII (1925), 112, n. 6; S. R. R., XVII (1925), 73, n. 7; S. R. R., XVI (1924), 72, n. 6; S. R. R., XIV (1922), 311, n. 7; S. R. R., XII (1920), 70, n. 11; S. R. R., VI (1914), 324, n. 1; S. R. R., IV (1912), 375-6, n. 1; S. R. R., III (1911), 243, n. 12; S. R. R., III (1911), 351, n. 11; *Fontes*, nn. 3282; 3363; 4211.

[83]Cf. S. R. R., XXIII (1931), 234, n. 20.

[84]Cf. S. R. R., XIX (1927), 175, n. 10.

cessity of living with disliked in-laws,[85] and the desire to conceal the fact of the marriage.[86] In one of the cases tried by the Rota the fact that the woman returned to her home shortly after the ceremony and lived with her parents for a time served to disprove rather than to substantiate the claim that she had simulated her consent. This was because the reason alleged for the simulation was her desire to liberate herself from parental authority.[87]

If the conjugal life of the consorts was extremely brief, there may be a good indication that it was not properly instituted inasmuch as it was so quickly dissolved.[88] This presumption will naturally be less compelling than in the case wherein there had been no cohabitation whatsoever, yet the Rota has frequently considered the early cessation of cohabitation as indicative of simulation in particular cases.[89]

On the contrary, an argument against the fact of simulation is had when the cohabitation of the consorts has endured for a lengthy period of time.[90] Regardless of whether the conjugal life had been speedily dissolved or protracted to some length, the reasons for its cessation may obviously be quite unrelated to any simulation of the original matrimonial consent. Of the various causes that may lead to the cessation of conjugal life, the following are met with frequently in the Rota Decisions: subsequent quarrels, adultery or suspected adultery, the enforced absences of the man, the ill health of one of the spouses, the dis-

---

85S. R. R., XXVIII (1936), 134, n. 9.

86Cf. S. R. R., XXVI (1934), 739, n. 19.

87S. R. R., XXIII (1931), 301, n. 16.

88S. R. R., XX (1928), 83, n. 3.

89Cf. S. R. R., XVIII (1926), 39, n. 14; S. R. R., XV (1923), 166, n. 1; S. R. R., XV (1923), 228, n. 11; S. R. R., XI (1919), 45, n. 11; S. R. R., VII (1915), 200, n. 8; S. R. R., V (1913), 215, n. 11; S. R. R., V (1913), 290-1, n. 14; S. R. R., III (1911), 330, n. 8; S. R. R., II (1910), 327-8, n. 16.

90Cf. *AAS*, XXXVI (1944), 196-7; S. R. R., XXVIII (1936), 11-12, n. 13; S. R. R., XXVIII (1936), 100, n. 1; S. R. R., XXVII (1935), 630, n. 25; S. R. R., XXV (1933), 83, n. 8; S. R. R., XXV (1933), 249, n. 14; S. R. R., XXIV (1932), 155, n. 7; S. R. R., XXII (1930), 201, n. 20; S. R. R., XXII (1930), 391, n. 12; S. R. R., XXI (1929), 210, n. 6; S. R. R., XXI (1929), 264, n. 10; S. R. R., XXI (1929), 551-2, n. 10; S. R. R., XX (1928), 247, n. 3; S. R. R., IV (1912), 405. n. 9; S. R. R., II (1910), 28, n. 10; S. R. R., II (1910), 160, n. 12.

appointment of one consort over the fact that no children were born, the dissolute character of a consort, temporary impotence, disappointment in the personality of the other spouse, or in the size of his fortune, the failure to discover a life of perfect bliss in marriage, the woman's inability to adapt herself to a lower standard of living, financial difficulties, and the consequences of a mixed marriage that was imprudently entered.[91] Causes of this nature may bring about in some cases a discontinuance of cohabitation within a very short time of the wedding, and yet it may be impossible to prove that the consent of either of the consorts had been fictitious at the moment of the ceremony.[92]

If it is established that the consort who is accused of total simulation believed his marriage to be valid at any time after the ceremony, there is a very grave indication that his consent was genuine, or at least that he was not guilty of total simulation.[93] The only possibility of proving total simulation in such a case seems to lie in the demonstration that the party was so influenced by fear that he was unable to declare with certainty whether or not he actually consented.[94] The obverse however does not hold, namely, even though it is proved that the party never considered himself married, it is not necessarily an indi-

---

[91]Cf. S. R. R., XXX (1938), 588, n. 5; S. R. R., XXX (1938), 645, n. 10; S. R. R., XXVI (1934), 77, n. 16; S. R. R., XXVI (1934), 171, n. 12; S. R. R., XXV (1933), 83, n. 8; S. R. R., XXV (1933), 249, n. 14; S. R. R., XXV (1933), 252, n. 19; S. R. R., XXV (1933), 396-7, nn. 23-25; S. R. R., XXV (1933), 454, n. 10; S. R. R., XXV (1933), 574-5, n. 11; S. R. R., XXIII (1931), 143-4, nn. 13-14; S. R. R., XXIII (1931), 201-2, n. 14; S. R. R., XXIII (1931), 234, n. 20; S. R. R., XXV (1933), 468, n. 11; S. R. R., XXII (1930), 474-5, n. 28; S. R. R., XXI (1929), 210, n. 6; S. R. R., XXI (1929), 551-2, n. 10; S. R. R., XVII (1925), 227, n. 9; S. R. R., XVII (1925), 378-9, nn. 8-9; S. R. R., XVI (1924), 321-2, n. 10; S. R. R., XV (1923), 25, n. 3; S. R. R., XII (1920), 46-7, n. 1; S. R. R., VIII (1916), 198, n. 3; S. R. R., VI (1914), 252, n. 18; S. R. R., IV (1912), 405, n. 9; S. R. R., IV (1912), 468, n. 22; S. R. R., II (1910), 160, n. 12.

[92]Cf. S. R. R., XXX (1938), 348-9, n. 9; S. R. R., XXX (1938), 351, n. 1; S. R. R., XXVII (1935), 551, n. 1; S. R. R., XXI (1929), 516, n. 12; S. R. R.,XVII (1925), 228, n. 18; S. R. R., XVI (1924), 321-2, n. 10.

[93]Cf. S. R. R., XXIX (1937), 533, n. 12; S. R. R., XXVIII (1936), 111, n. 11; S R. R., XXVII (1935), 101, n. 3; S. R. R., XXV (1933), 84, n. 8; S. R. R., XXV (1933), 249, n. 14; S. R. R., XXIII (1931), 141, n. 7; S. R. R., XXII (1930), 475, n. 29; S. R. R., XXI (1929), 551-2, n. 10; S. R. R., II (1910), 160, n. 12; *AAS*, XXXVI (1944), 196-7.

[94]Cf. S. R. R., XIX (1927), 316, n. 3.

cation that his consent was defective.[95] The fact that the party regretted having married perhaps indicates that he was less free in consenting to the marriage, but not that he actually simulated the consent to which he gave external expression.[96]

Marital infidelity on the part of one of the spouses in the early days of marriage, though usually of greater probative value in cases of partial simulation, may likewise provide adminicular proof that the consent was totally simulated.[97] An absolute disregard for conjugal fidelity, and also the continuation of a dissolute manner of living, may well indicate that the consent to the marriage was fictitious, provided that an adequate cause for the simulation has been proved.[98] The prorogation of such a state of affairs for a lengthy period of time may reveal however that the party considered himself bound to an unfortunate marriage, and thus disprove the existence of at least a total simulation.[99]

When adultery did not occur until some time after the marriage, it would be of little value as an indication of simulation, since it can then be more readily accounted for through the usual causes.[100]

The continuation of sinful relations with others in spite of the celebration of the marriage is not necessarily an indication of simulation.[101] When these relations took place with the same person, both before and after the ceremony, the adminicular evidence thereby provided may be of somewhat greater value,[102] though never would it constitute apodictic proof.[103]

95"Scientia aut opinio nullitatis matrimonii consensum matrimonialem necessario non excludit."—Canon 1085.

96S. R. R., XXIX (1937), 318, n. 6; S. R. R., XVII (1925), 378, n. 8.

97Cf. S. R. R., XX (1928), 396-7, n. 11; S. R. R., XV (1923), 165-173.

98Cf. S. R. R., XXVI (1934), 469-472, nn. 5-9; S. R. R., XXIII (1931), 83-85, nn. 18-19; S. R. R., VII (1915), 200 n. 8; S. R. R., XI (1919), 44-5, n. 10; S. R. R., III (1911), 24-6, nn. 15-16.

99Cf. S. R. R., XVI (1924), 321-2, n. 10.

100Cf. S. R. R., XXV (1933), 454, n. 10; S. R. R., XXV (1933), 468, n. 11; S. R. R., XXIII (1931), 304, n. 21; S. R. R., XVII (1925), 375, n. 4.

101". . . .asperitas viri immo et fidelitatis fractio in ipso initio vitae coniugalis, licet magnopere reprobrandae, non sunt certum argumentum simulationis consensus."—S. R. R., XVII (1925), 228, n. 18. Cf. also S. R. R., XVII (1925), 379, n. 9.

102Cf. S. R. R., XX (1928), 396-7, n. 11; S. R. R., VII (1915), 200, n. 8; S. R. R., IV (1912), 468, n. 22; S. R. R., III (1911) 351, n. 11.

103Cf. S. R. R., XXIII (1931), 234, n. 20; S. R. R., XVIII (1926), 265, n. 9.

The exclusion of the blessing of offspring (*intentio non sese obligandi)* does not nullify matrimonial consent unless it was introduced into the contract at the time of the ceremony.[104] Although the continual practice of onanism is by no means a necessary indication of spurious consent, it may nevertheless provide adminicular evidence of this when it is accompanied with other and more cogent arguments that point to a total simulation.[105]

Not infrequently it happens that a consort who is accused of simulating marital consent became converted to Catholicism and received baptism before the marriage. If this has occurred in a particular case, an additional source of evidence may be available to the judge.

When it has been established that the party was sincere in embracing the true faith, there appears to be a grave indication that his matrimonial consent was equally sincere.[106] That he possessed the proper intention in submitting to baptism may be demonstrated, for example, by his reception of the sacrament of confirmation after the marriage, or by the fact that he has remained a faithful Catholic in spite of the unfortunate outcome of his marriage.[107] Conversely, proof that the conversion was simulated may provide a basis for the presumption that the matrimonial consent was also fictitious.[108]

With regard to the claim that a marriage was contracted merely as a joke, it will be sufficient to note that this contention becomes disproved as soon as there is established the fact that the parties lived together in mutual affection and harmony, even though only for a short time.[109]

---

[104]Griese, *The Marriage Contract and the Procreation of Offspring*, pp. 86-88.

[105]Cf. S. R. R., XXIV (1932), 76, n. 13; S. R. R., VII (1915), 200, n. 8; S. R. R., III (1911), 24-26, nn. 15-16.

[106]Cf. S. R. R., VI (1914), 247, n. 7.

[107]Cf. S. R. R., XXVI (1934), 678, n. 14.

[108]Cf. S. R. R., XXI (1929), 238, n. 14; S. R. R., VII (1915), 200, n. 8.

[109]S. R. R., XXX (1938), 587-8, n. 4.

CONCLUSIONS

I. A marriage that is invalid on the ground of total simulation cannot be simultaneously null on account of the total absence of consent, or the lack of a sufficient manifestation of consent, of force and fear, of unfulfilled condition, or of the exclusion of an essential marital obligation. Consequently a tribunal cannot declare a marriage invalid on account of the total simulation of consent and at the same time on the ground of one of these other species of deficient consent. Page 34.

II. When it has been established by proof that the postulated conditions of canon 1087 existed in a particular case, the marriage may be declared invalid, even though it cannot be determined whether or not the party actually consented to marry. Page 73.

III. The complete definition of *tempus non suspectum as* given by the Instruction of the Sacred Congregation of the Sacraments of the year 1923 is not applicable in cases of total simulation. *Tempus non suspectum* in these cases refers to that period of time when no reasons existed which would have urged a consort to state a falsehood by declaring that his consent was fictious. Page 62.

IV. Any manifestation by the simulator of the fact that a fictitious consent was given, be it only by acts or deeds, may rightly be considered an extra-judicial confession of simulation. Page 60.

V. In the cases brought before the Rota the most frequently alleged causes of total simulation are fear, the desire for the satisfaction of lust, and the desire for financial gain. Page 75.

VI. The proof of the fact of total simulation necessitates the proof of the existence of an aversion on the part of the alleged simulator towards the other consort or at least towards marriage with that consort, and it must furthermore be shown that this aversion existed at the time of the wedding. When it has been established that a party cherished a marital affection for the other consort shortly before and after the wedding, there is a grave indication that his marital consent was not simulated. Page 87.

VII. An aversion on the part of a consort towards the circumstances of the wedding is not the aversion referred to in the preceding conclusion. Page 69.

VIII. A fear justly inflicted, *ab intrinseco,* and only subjectively grave, may provide a sufficient cause of simulation. Page 74.

IX. When it has been established that the alleged simulator feigned conversion to the Catholic Church before marriage, there is an indication that his matrimonial consent was also feigned, provided that a cause of the simulation is in evidence and the circumstances of the case do not contradict this conclusion. Page 94.

X. Hesitation and reluctance in consenting to marriage or the shedding of tears in doing so most frequently indicate a genuine rather than a fictious consent. Page 85.

XI. Since total simulation implies the positive intention of not contracting marriage, the party who has totally simulated matrimonial consent is fully aware of his act and knows that his marriage is invalid. Consequently the proof of the fact that a person considered himself as truly married at any time after the wedding precludes the possibility that he has totally simulated matrimonial consent. The only exception to this conclusion is the case wherein a party submitted to the wedding ceremony because of duress, and was so emotionally disturbed that afterwards he could not state with certitude whether or not he actually consented to marry. Page 19.

XII. With the exception of the case wherein total simution was motivated by lust, the prompt and frequent consummation of the marriage constitutes a grave indication that the matrimonial consent was genuine. On the contrary, when the marriage was not consummated, or when the consummation was delayed or infrequent, this may well be indicative of spurious consent. Pages 87-88.

XIII. Flight from the other consort immediately after the ceremony constitutes a very grave indication that a party's marital consent was not genuine. Page 89.

XIV. Usually a man who simulates marital consent in order to carnally possess a woman deserts her after a short period; similarly the person who simulates consent for financial gain has no purpose in continuing the deception after the end has been attained. Page 72.

XV. A lengthy period of cohabitation provides an indication that the matrimonial consent was not feigned, whereas a very brief period of cohabitation may well be an indication that the marriage was not properly instituted. Page 91.

ALPHABETICAL INDEX

BIBLIOGRAPHY

Sources

Acta Apostolicae Sedis, Commentarium Officiale, Romae, 1909-.

Acta et Decreta Sacrorum Conciliorum Recentiorum, Collectio Lacensis, 7 vols., Friburgi Brisgoviae: Herder, 1870-1890.

Bouscaren, T. Lincoln, *The Canon Law Digest*, 2 vols., Milwaukee: Bruce, 1934-1943.

Canons and Decrees of the Council of Trent, ed. H. J. Schroeder, St. Louis: Herder, 1941.

Canones et Decreta Concilii Tridentini, editio Neopolitana Joseph Palella, Neapoli, 1859.

Codex Iuris Canonici Pii X Pontificis Maximi iussa digestus Benedicti XV auctoritate promulgatus, Romae: Typis Polyglottis Vaticanis, 1917; reimpressio, 1934.

Codicis Iuris Canonici Fontes, cura Emi. Petri Card. Gasparri editi, 9 vols., Romae (postea Civitate Vaticana): Typis Polyglottis Vaticanis, 1923-1939 (Vols. VII, VIII, et IX ed. cura et studio Emi. Iustiniani Card. Serédi).

Collectanea S. Congregationis de Propaganda Fide, 2 vols., Romae: ex Typographia Polyglotta Vaticana, 1907.

Corpus Iuris Canonici, ed. Lipsiensis secunda post Aemilii Ludovici Richter curas instruxit Aemilius Friedberg, 2 vols., Lipsiae, 1879-1881. Editio anastitice repetita, Lipsiae: Tauchnitz, 1928.

Corpus Iuris Civilis, 3 vols. Berolini: Apud Weidmannas, 1928-1929.
Vol. I, ed. stereotypa 15., *Institutiones*, quas recognovit et retractavit P. Krueger.
Vol. I, ed. stereotypa 15., *Digesta*, quae recognovit et retractavit P. Krueger.
Vol. II, ed. stereotypa 10., *Codex Iustinianus*, quem recognovit et retractavit P. Krueger.
Vol. III ed. stereotypa 5., *Novellae*, quas recognovit R. Schoell, et absolvit G. Kroll.

Decretales D. Gregorii Papae IX, una cum Glossis Restitutae, Romae: 1582.

Decretum Gratiani, una cum Glossis Gregorii XIII Pont. Max. iussu editum, Romae, 1582.

Denzinger, H.—Bannwart, C.—Umberg, J., *Enchiridion Symbolorum Definitionum et Declarationum de Rebus Fidei et Morum*, 21.-23. ed., Friburgi-Brisgoviae: Herder, 1937.

Friedberg, *Quinque Compilationes Antiquae* (Lipsiae 1882).

Jaffé, P., *Regesta Pontificum Romanorum ab condita Ecclesiae ad annum post Christum natum MCXCVIII*, 2. ed., 2 vols., Lipsiae, 1885-1888.

Mansi, J., *Sacrorum Conciliorum Nova et Amplissima Collectio*, 53 vols. in 60, Parisiis, 1901-1927.

Poste, Edward, *Gaii Institutiones*, Oxford, 1904.

Potthast, A., *Regesta Pontificum Romanorum inde ab anno post Christum natum MCXCVIII ad annum MCCCIV*, 2 vols., Berolini, 1874-1875.

Sacrae Romanae Rotae Decisiones seu Sententiae quae iuxta Legem Propriam et Constitutionem "Sapienti Consilio" Pii PP. X prodierunt, cura eiusdem S. Tribunalis editae, Romae: Typis Polyglottis Vaticanis, 1912—.

Thesaurus Resolutionum Sacrae Congregationis Concilii, 167 vols., Romae 1718-1908.

Authors

Aquinas, S. Thomas, *Summa Theologica*, 6 vols., Taurini: Marietti, 1937.

———, *The Summa Theologica of Saint Thomas Aquinas, literally translated by the Fathers of the English Dominican Province*, 22 vols., London: Burns-Oates and Washbourne, Ltd., 1912-1936.

Ayrinhac, H. A.—Lydon, P. J. *Marriage Legislation in the New Code of Canon Law*, revised edition, New York: Benziger Brothers, 1932.

Bangen, Ioannes H., *Instructio Practica de Sponsalibus et Matrimonio in usum Sacerdotum Curatorum*, Aschendorffianae, 1858-1860.

Bayón, J. Garcia F., *Tractatus Canonico-Moralis de Sacramento Matrimonii*, 2 vols. in 1, ed. 1931, Madrid: Editorial del C. de Maria.

Benedictus XIV (Prosper Lambertini), *De Synodo Diocesana*, libri 13 in 2 tom., Romae, 1806.

Bohic, Henricus, *In Quinque Decretalium Libros Commentaria*, Venetiis, 1576.

Bonaventura, S., *Commentaria in Quattuor Libros Sententiarum Petri Lombardi, Doctoris Seraphici S. Bonaventurae S. R. E. Cardinalis, Opera Omnia*, 10 vols., ed. Quaracchi, 1882-1902.

Bouscaren, T. Lincoln-Ellis, Adam C., *Canon Law*, Milwaukee: Bruce, 1946.

Cappello, Felix M., *Tractus Canonico-Moralis de Sacramentis*, 3 vols. in 6, Vol. III, *De Matrimonio*, 4 ed., 1939, Romae: Marietti.

Catholic Encyclopedia, The, 15 vols. with Index and 2 Supplements, New York, 1907-1922.

Chelodi, Ioannes, *Ius Canonicum de Matrimonio*, 5 ed. recognita et aucta a Pio Ciprotti, Vincenza: Società Anonima Tipografica Editrice, 1947.

Coronata, Matthaeus Conte a, *Institutiones Iuris Canonici, Tractatus Canonicus de Sacramentis*, 3 vols., Romae: Marietti, 1943-1946.

Corpus Scriptorum Ecclesiasticorum Latinorum, 71 vols., Pragae, Vindobonae, Lipsiae, 1866-.

D'Annibale, Iosephuus, *Summula Theologiae Moralis*, 3. ed., 3 vols., Romae, 1888-1892.

De Angelis, Phillipus, *Praelectiones Iuris Canonici ad Methodum Decretalium Gregorii IX Exactae*, 9 vols., Romae-Parisiis, 1877-1891.

De Becker, Iulius, *De Sponsalibus et Matrimonio Praelectiones Canonicae*, Bruxellis, 1896.

De Lugo, Ioannes, *Disputationes Scholasticae et Morales*, nova ed., J. B. Fournials, 8 vols., Parisiis, 1868-1869.

De Smet, Aloysius, *Tractatus Theologico- Canonicus de Sponsalibus et Matrimonio*, 4. ed., Brugis: Car. Beyaert, 1927.

Doheny, William, *Canonical Procedure in Matrimonial Cases*, Vol. I, *Formal Procedure*, Vol. II, *Informal Procedure*, Milwaukee: Bruce, 1938, 1944.

Esmein, A. -Génestal, R. -Dauvillier, J., *Le Mariage en Droit Canonique*, 2. ed., 2 vols., Paris, 1929-1935.

Fagnanus, Prosper, *Commentaria in Quinque Libros Decretalium*, 5 vols. in 3, Venetiis, 1708.

Ferraris, Lucius, *Prompta Bibliotheca Canonica, Iuridica, Moralis, Theologica necnon Ascetica, Polemica, Rubricistica, Historica*, 9 vols., Romae, 1885-1899.

Gasparri, Petrus Card., *Tractatus Canonicus de Matriminio*, ed. nova ad mentem Codicis I. C., 2 vols., Romae: Typis Polyglottis Vaticanis, 1932.

————, *Tractatus Canonicus de Matrimonio*, 3. ed., 2 vols., Paris, 1904.

Glynn, John C., *The Promoter of Justice*, The Catholic University of America Canon Law Studies, n. 101, Washington, D. C.: The Catholic University of America, 1936.

Gonzales-Tellez, Emmanuel, *Commentaria Perpetua in Singulos Textus Quinque Librorum Decretalium Gregorii IX*, 5 vols. in 4, Venetiis, 1699.

Griese, N. Orville, *The Marriage Contract and the Procreation of Offspring*, The Catholic University of America Canon Law Studies, n. 226, Washington, D.C.: The Catholic University of America Press, 1946.

Heylen, V., *Tractatus de Matrimonio*, ed. nona, Mechliniae: H. Dessain, 1945.

Hostiensis, Cardinalis (Henricus de Segusio), *Commentaria in Quinque Libros Decretalium*, 5 vols. in 3, Venetiis, 1581.

————, *Summa Aurea*, Lugduni, 1568.

Lancelotti, Paulus, *Institutiones Iuris Canonici*, Lugduni, 1579.

Laymann, Paul, *Theologia Moralis*, 6. ed., 2 vols., Bambergae, 1669.

Leclercq, Jacques, *Marriage and the Family*, trans. by Thomas R. Hanley, New York and Cincinnati: Pustet, 1945.

Liguori, S. Alphonsus M. de, *Theologia Moralis*, cura et studio P. Gaudé, 4 vols., Romae, 1905-1912.

Lombard, Peter, *Sententiarum Libri Quattuor*, ed. Migne, Paris, 1853.

Merkelbach, Benedictus H., *Summa Theologiae Moralis*, 3. ed., 3 vols., Parisiis: De Brouwer et Soc., 1939.

Migne, Jacques Paul, *Patrologiae Cursus Completus, Series Graeca*, 161 vols., Parisiis, 1856-1866.

————, *Patrologiae Curus Completus, Series Latina*, 221 vols., Parisiis, 1844-1864.

McSorley, Joseph, *An Outline History of the Church by Centuries*, St. Louis: Herder, 1945.

Panormitanus, Abbas (Nicolaus de Tudeschis), *Commentaris in Quinque Libros Decretalium*, 5 vols in 7, Venetiis, 1588.

Payen, G., *De Matrimonio in Missionibus ac Potissimum in Sinis Tractatus Practicus et Casus*, 2. ed., 3 vols., Zi-ka-wei: in typographia T'Ou-Se-We, 1935-1936.

Pichler, Vitus, *Epitome Iuris Canonici*, 2 vols., Venetiis, 1755.

Pirhing, Ernricus, *Ius Canonicum in Quinque Libros Decretalium Distributum Nova Methodo Explicatum*, 5 vols. in 4, Dilingae, 1674-1678.

Plauché, Charles, *Simulated Matrimonial Consent*, Washington: The Catholic University of America, 1942 (Licentiate Dissertation, not printed).

Raymond of Pennafort, St., *Summa*, Veronae, 1744.

Reiffenstuel, Anacletus, *Ius Canonicum Universum*, 5 vols. in 7, Parisiis, 1864-1870.

Roberti, Franciscus, *De Processibus*, 2 vols., Romae: Apud Aedes Facultatis Iuridicae ad S. Apollinaris, 1926; Vol. I, 2. ed., Romae: Apud Custodiam Librariam Pontificii Instituti Utriusque Iuris, 1941.

Rommen, Heinrich A., *The Natural Law*, trans. by Thomas R. Hanley, St. Louis: Herder, 1947.

Rufinus, *Summa Decretorum*, ed. H. Singer, Paderborn, 1902.

Sanchez, Thomas, *Disputationum de Sancto Matrimonii Sacramento Tomi Tres*, 3 vols., Venetiis, 1726.

Sangmeister, Joseph V., *Force and Fear as Precluding Matrimonial Consent*, The Catholic University of America Canon Law Studies, n. 80, Washington, D.C.: The Catholic University of America, 1932.

Santi, Franciscus, *Praelectiones Iuris Canonici iuxta Ordinem Decretalium Gregorii IX*, 2 vols., Ratisbonae, Neo-Eboraci, Cincinnati, 1886.

Schmalzgrueber, Franciscus, *Ius Ecclesiasticum Universum*, 5 vols in 12, Romae, 1843-1845.

Schulte, J. F. von, *Die Geschichte der Quellen und Literatur des Canonischen Rechts*, 3 vols., Stuttgart, 1875-1880.

Suarez, Franciscus, *Opera Omnia*, 28 vols., Parisiis, 1856-1878.

Timlin, Bartholomew, *Conditional Matrimonial Consent*, The Catholic University of America Canon Law Studies, n. 89, Washington, D.C.: The Catholic University of America, 1934.

Wanenmacher, Francis, *Canonical Evidence in Marriage Cases*, Philadelphia: Dolphin Press, 1935.

Van Bogaert, Edward, *Simulated Matrimonial Consent*, Washington: The Catholic University of America, 1939 (Licentiae dissertation not printed).

Van Hove, A., *Commentarium Lovaniense in Codicem Iuris Canonici*, Vol. I, Tomus I, *Prolegomena ad Codicem Iuris Canonici*, 2. ed., Mechliniae-Romae: H. Dessain, 1945.

Vermeersch, A. -Creusen, I., *Epitome Iuris Canonici*, 3 vols., 5. ed., Mechliniae: H. Dessain, 1933-1936.

Wernz, F. X., *Ius Decretalium*, 2. ed., Romae et Prati, 1906-1913.

Wernz, F. S. -Vidal, P., *Ius Canonicum*, 7 vols. in 8, Romae: apud Aedes Universitatis Gregorianae, 1923-1938.

Articles

Donnelly, Francis B., "Fraud and the Estoppel of Canon 1971, § 1, n. 1"—*The Jurist*, VI (1946), 378-400.

Kelly, James P., "Force and Fear Affecting Matrimonial Consent—*The Jurist*, V (1945), 514-532.

Kuttner, S., "The 'glossa ordinaria' to the Gregorian Decretals"—*The English Historical Review*, LX (1945), 97-105.

Pellegrini, B., "De Intentione Bono Sacramenti Adversa Eiusdemque Probatione in Iudicio ad Norman Can. 1086"—*Jus Pontificium*, IX (1929), 306-311.

Quinn, Andrew, "Defects in Marriage Consent"—*The Jurist*, V (1945), 532-551.

Reh, Francis F., "Guilt of the Plaintiff in a Marriage Case"—*The Jurist*, III (1943), 404-415.

Roberti, F., "De Matrimonii Accusatione"—*Apollinaris*, VI (1933), 441-444.

Roberti, F., "Quaestiones quaedam de identificatione actionum ob vitia consensus in causis matrimonialibus"—*Apollinaris*, VI (1933), 105-107.

Wanenmacher, Francis, "Some questions on vitiated marital consent"—*The Ecclesiastical Review*, C (1939), 481-497; CI (1939), 31-49; CI (1939), 131-149.

Periodicals

Apollinaris, Romae, 1928—.

American Ecclesiastical Review, The, Vols. I-XXXII, 1889-1905, Philadelphia; *Ecclesiastical Review, The*, Vols. XXXIII-CIX, 1905-1943, Philadelphia; *American Ecclesiastical Review, The*, Vol. CX—, 1944-, Washington, D.C.

English Historical Review, The, London: Longmans Green & Co., 1886-

Jurist, The, Washington, D.C., 1941-

Jus Pontificium, Romae, 1921-1940.

BIOGRAPHICAL NOTE

Basil Francis Courtemanche was born in Toronto, Ontario, February 5, 1919. He attended Saint Brigid's Separate School and De La Salle "Oaklands" High School for boys. In September, 1938, he entered Saint Augustine's Seminary, Toronto, where he received the B.A. degree from the University of Toronto in June, 1941. He was ordained to the Holy Priesthood on May 26, 1945, and enrolled in the School of Canon Law of the Catholic University of America in September, 1945. He received the degree of the Baccalaureate in Canon Law in June, 1946, and the degree of the Licentiate in Canon Law in June, 1947.

CANON LAW STUDIES*

1. FRERIKS, REV. CELESTINE A., C.PP.S., J.C.D., Religious Congregations in Their External Relations, 121 pp., 1916.
2. GALLIHER, REV. DANIEL M., O.P., J.C.D., Canonical Elections, 117 pp. 1917.
3. BORKOWSKI, REV. AURELIUS L., O.F.M., J.C.D., De Confraternitatibus Ecclesiasticis, 136 pp., 1918.
4. CASTILLO, REV. CAYO, J.C.D., Disertacion Historico-Canonica sobre la Potestad del Cabildo en Sede Vacante o Impedida del Vicario Capitular, 99 pp., 1919 (1918).
5. KUBELBECK, REV. WILLIAM J., S.T.B.; J.C.D., The Sacred Penitentiaria and Its Relation to Faculties of Ordinaries and Priests, 129 pp., 1918.
6. PETROVITS, REV. JOSEPH J. C., S.T.D., J.C.D., The New Church Law on Matrimony, X-461 pp., 1919.
7. HICKEY, REV. JOHN J., S.T.B., J.C.D., Irregularities and Simple Impediments in the New Code of Canon Law, 100 pp., 1920.
8. KLEKOTKA, REV. PETER J., S.T.B., J.C.D., Diocesan Consultors, 179 pp., 1920.
9. WANENMACHER, REV. FRANCIS, J.C.D., The Evidence in Ecclesiastical Procedure Affecting the Marriage Bond, 1920 (Printed 1935).
10. GOLDEN, REV. HENRY FRANCIS, J.C.D., Parochial Benefices in the New Code, IV-119 pp., 1921 (Printed 1925).
11. KOUDELKA, REV. CHARLES J., J.C.D., Pastors, Their Rights and Duties According to the New Code of Canon Law, 211 pp., 1921.
12. MELO, REV. ANTONIUS, O.F.M., J.C.D., De Exemptions Regularium, X-188 pp., 1921.
13. SCHAAF, REV. VALENTINE THEODORE, O.F.M., S.T.B., J.C.D., The Cloister, X-180 pp., 1921.
14. BURKE, REV. THOMAS JOSEPH, S.T.D., J.C.D., Competence in Ecclesiastical Tribunals, IV-117 pp., 1922.
15. LEECH, REV. GEORGE LEO, J.C.D., A Comparative Study of the Constitution "Apostolicae Sedis" and the "Codex Juris Canonici," 179 pp., 1922.
16. MOTRY, REV. HUBERT LOUIS, S.T.D., J.C.D., Diocesan Faculties According to the Code of Canon Law, II-167 pp., 1922.
17. MURPHY, REV. GEORGE LAWRENCE, J.C.D., Delinquencies and Penalties in the Administration and the Reception of the Sacraments, IV-121 pp., 1923.
18. O'REILLY, REV. JOHN ANTHONY, S.T.B., J.C.D., Ecclesiastical Sepulture in the New Code of Canon Law, II-129 pp., 1923.

*Below n. 100 only the following numbers are still available: Nn. 3, 4, 9, 25, 34, 57 and 75. Beginning with n. 100 only the following are unavailable: Nn. 100-111 inclusive and n. 113.

19. Michalicka, Rev. Wenceslas Cyril, O.S.B., J.C.D., Judicial Procedure in Dismissal of Clerical Exempt Religious, 107 pp., 1923.
20. Dargin, Rev. Edward Vincent, S.T.B., J.C.D., Reserved Cases According to the Code of Canon Law, IV-103 pp., 1924.
21. Godfrey, Rev. John A., S.T.B., J.C.D., The Right of Patronage According to the Code of Canon Law, 153 pp., 1924.
22. Hagedorn, Rev. Francis Edward, J.C.D., General Legislation on Indulgences, II-154 pp., 1924.
23. King, Rev. James Ignatius, J.C.D., The Administration of the Sacraments to Dying Catholics, V-141 pp., 1924.
24. Winslow, Rev. Francis Joseph, O.F.M., J.C.D., Vicars and Prefects Apostolic, IV-149 pp., 1924.
25. Correa, Rev. Jose Servelion, S.T.L., J.C.D., La Potestad Legislativa de la Iglesia Catolica IV-127 pp., 1925.
26. Dugan, Rev. Henry Francis, A.M., J.C.D., The Judiciary Department of the Diocesan Curia, 87 pp., 1925.
27. Keller, Rev. Charles Frederick, S.T.B., J.C.D., Mass Stipends, 167 pp., 1925.
28. Paschang, Rev. John Linus, J.C.D., The Sacramentals According to the Code of Canon Law, 129 pp., 1925.
29. Piontek, Rev. Cyrillus, O.F.M., S.T.B., J.C.D., De Indulto Exclaustrationis necnon Saecularizationis, XIII-289 pp., 1925.
30. Kearney, Rev. Richard Joseph, S.T.B., J.C.D., Sponsors at Baptism According to the Code of Canon Law, IV-127 pp., 1925.
31. Bartlett, Rev. Chester Joseph, A.M., LL.B., J.C.D., The Tenure of Parochial Property in the United States of America, V-108 pp., 1926.
32. Kilker, Rev. Adrian Jerome, J.C.D., Extreme Unction, V-425 pp., 1926.
33. McCormick, Rev. Robert Emmett, J.C.D., Confessors of Religious, VIII-266 pp., 1926.
34. Miller, Rev. Newton Thomas, J.C.D., Founded Masses According to the Code of Canon Law, VII-93 pp., 1926.
35. Roelker, Rev. Edward G., S.T.D., J.C.D., Principles of Privilege According to the Code of Canon Law, XI-166 pp., 1926.
36. Bakalarczyk, Rev. Richardus, M.I.C., J.U.D., De Novitiatu, VIII-208 pp. 1927.
37. Pizzuti, Rev. Lawrence, O.F.M., J.U.L., De Parochis Religiosis, 1927. (Not Printed.)
38. Bliley, Rev. Nicholas Martin, O.S.B., J.C.D., Altars According to the Code of Canon Law, XIX-132 pp., 1927.
39. Brown, Mr. Brendan Francis, A.B., LL.M., J.U.D., The Canonical Juristic Personality with Special Reference to its Status in the United States of America, V-212 pp., 1927.
40. Cavanaugh, Rev. William Thomas, C.P., J.U.D., The Reservation of the Blessed Sacrament, VIII-101 pp., 1927.
41. Doheny, Rev. William J., C.S.C., A.B., J.U.D., Church Property: Modes of Acquisition, X-118 pp., 1927.
42. Feldhaus, Rev. Aloysius H., C.PP.S., J.C.D., Oratories, IX-141 pp., 1927.

43. KELLY, REV. JAMES PATRICK, A.B., J.C.D., The Jurisdiction of the Simple Confessor, X-208 pp., 1927.
44. NEUBERGER, REV. NICHOLAS J., J.C.D., Canon 6 or the Relation of the Codex Juris Canonici to the Preceding Legislation, V-95 pp., 1927.
45. O'KEEFE, REV. GERALD MICHAEL, J.C.D., Matrimonial Dispensations, Powers of Bishops, Priests, and Confessors, VIII-232 pp., 1927.
46. QUIGLEY, REV. JOSEPH A. M., A.B., J.C.D., Condemned Societies, 139 pp., 1927.
47. ZAPLOTNIK, REV. JOHANNES LEO, J.C.D., De Vicariis Foraneis, X-142 pp., 1927.
48. DUSKIE, REV. JOHN ALOYSIUS, A.B., J.C.D., The Canonical Status of the Orientals in the United States, VIII-196 pp., 1928.
49. HYLAND, REV. FRANCIS EDWARD, J.C.D., Excommunication, Its Nature, Historical Development and Effects, VIII-181 pp., 1928.
50. REINMANN, REV. GERALD JOSEPH, O.M.C., J.C.D., The Third Order Secular of Saint Francis, 201 pp., 1928.
51. SCHENK, REV. FRANCIS J., J.C.D., The Matrimonial Impediments of Mixed Religion and Disparity of Cult, XVI-318 pp., 1929.
52. COADY, REV. JOHN JOSEPH, S.T.D., J.U.D., A.M., The Appointment of Pastors, VIII-150 pp., 1929.
53. KAY, REV. THOMAS HENRY, J.C.D., Competence in Matrimonial Procedure, VIII-164 pp., 1929.
54. TURNER, REV. SIDNEY JOSEPH, C.P., J.U.D., The Vow of Poverty XLIX-217 pp., 1929.
55. KEARNEY, REV. RAYMOND A., A.B., S.T.D., J.C.D., The Principles of Delegation, VII-149 pp., 1929.
56. CONRAN, REV. EDWARD JAMES, A.B., J.C.D., The Interdict, V-163 pp., 1930.
57. O'NEILL, REV. WILLIAM H., J.C.D., Papal Rescripts of Favor, VII-218 pp., 1930.
58. BASTNAGEL, REV. CLEMENT VINCENT, J.U.D., The Appointment of Parochial Adjutants and Assistants, XV-257 pp., 1930.
59. FERRY, REV. WILLIAM A., A.B., J.C.D., Stole Fees, V-136 pp., 1930.
60. COSTELLO, REV. JOHN MICHAEL, A.B., J.C.D., Domicile and Quasi-Domicile,VII-201 pp., 1930.
61. KREMER, REV. MICHAEL NICHOLAS, A.B., S.T.B., J.C.D., Church Support in the United States, VI-136 pp., 1930.
62. ANGULO, REV. LUIS, C.M., J.C.D., Legislation de la Iglesia sobre la intencion en la application de la Santa Misa, VII-104 pp., 1931.
63. FREY, REV. WOLFGANG NORBERT, O.S.B., A.B., J.C.D., The Act of Religious Profession, VIII-174 pp., 1931.
64. ROBERTS, REV. JAMES BRENDAN, A.B., J.C.D., The Banns of Marriage, XIV-104 pp., 1931.
65. RYDER, REV. RAYMOND ALOYSIUS, A.B., J.C.D., Simony, IX-151 pp., 1931.
66. CAMPAGNA, REV. ANGELO, PH.D., J.U.D., Il Vicario Generale del Vescovo, VII-205 pp., 1931.

67 Cox, Rev. Joseph Godfrey, A.B., J.C.D., The Administration of Seminaries, VI-124 pp., 1931.

68. Gregory, Rev. Donald J., J.U.D., The Pauline Privilege, XV-165 pp., 1931.

69. Donohue, Rev. John F., J.C.D., The Impediment of Crime, VII-110 pp., 1931.

70. Dooley, Rev. Eugene A., O.M.I., J.C.D., Church Law on Sacred Relics IX-143 pp., 1931.

71. Orth, Rev. Clement Raymond, O.M.C., J.C.D., The Approbation of Religious Institutes, 171 pp., 1931.

72. Pernicone, Rev. Joseph M., A.B., J.C.D., The Ecclesiastical Prohibition of Books, XII-267 pp., 1932.

73. Clinton, Rev. Connell, A.B., J.C.D., The Paschal Precept, IX-108 pp., 1932.

74. Donnelly, Rev. Francis B., A.M., S.T.L., J.C.D., The Diocesan Synod, VIII-125 pp., 1932.

75. Torrente, Rev. Camilo, C.M.F., J.C.D., Las Procesiones Sagradas, V-145 pp., 1932.

76. Murphy, Rev. Edwin J., C.PP.S., J.C.D., Suspension Ex Informata Conscientia, XI-122 pp., 1932.

77. MacKenzie, Rev. Eric F., A.M., S.T.L., J.C.D., The Delict of Heresy in its Commission, Penalization, Absolution, VII-124 pp., 1932.

78. Lyons, Rev. Avitus E., S.T.B., J.C.D., The Collegiate Tribunal of First Instance, XI-147 pp., 1932.

79. Connolly, Rev. Thomas A., J.C.D., Appeals, XI-195 pp., 1932.

80. Sangmeister, Rev. Joseph V., A.B., J.C.D., Force and Fear as Precluding Matrimonial Consent, V-211 pp., 1932.

81. Jaeger, Rev. Leo A., A.B., J.C.D., The Administration of Vacant and Quasi-Vacant Episcopal Sees in the United States, IX-229 pp., 1932.

82. Rimlinger, Rev. Herbert T. J.C.D., Error Invalidating Matrimonial Consent, VII-79 pp., 1932.

83. Barrett, Rev. John D. M., S.S., J.C.D., A Comparative Study of the Third Plenary Council of Baltimore and the Code, IX-221 pp., 1932.

84. Carberry, Rev. John J., Ph.D., S.T.D., J.C.D., The Juridical Form of Marriage, X-177 pp., 1934.

85. Dolan, Rev. John L., A.B., J.C.D., The Defensor Vinculi, XII-157 pp., 1934.

86. Hannan, Rev. Jerome D., A.M., S.T.D., LL.B., J.C.D., The Canon Law of Wills, IX-517 pp., 1934.

87. Lemieux, Rev. Delise A., A.M., J.C.D., The Sentence in Ecclesiastical Procedure, IX-131 pp., 1934.

88. O'Rourke, Rev. James J., A.B., J.C.D., Parish Registers, VII-109 pp., 1934.

89. Timlin, Rev. Bartholomew, O.F.M., A.M., J.C.D., Conditional Matrimonial Consent, X-381 pp., 1934.

90. Wahl, Rev. Francis X., A.B., J.C.D., The Matrimonial Impediments of Consanguinity and Affinity, VI-125 pp., 1934.

91. White, Rev. Robert J., A.B., LL.B., S.T.B., J.C.D., Canonical Ante-Nuptial Promises and the Civil Law, VI-152 pp., 1934.
92. Herrera, Rev. Antonio Parra, O.C.D., J.C.D., Legislacion Eclesiastica sobra el Ayuno y la Abstinencia, XI-191 pp., 1935.
93. Kennedy, Rev. Edwin J., J.C.D., The Special Matrimonial Process in Cases of Evident Nullity, X-165 pp., 1935.
94. Manning, Rev. John J., A.B., J.C.D., Presumption of Law in Matrimonial Procedure, XI-111 pp., 1935.
95. Moeder, Rev. John M., J.C.D., The Proper Bishop for Ordination and Dimissorial Letters, VII-135 pp., 1935.
96. O'Mara, Rev. William A., A.B., J.C.D., Canonical Causes for Matrimonial Dispensations, IX-155 pp., 1935.
97. Reilly, Rev. Peter, J.C.D., Residence of Pastors, IX-81 pp., 1935.
98. Smith, Rev. Mariner T., O.P., S.T.Lr., J.C.D., The Penal Law for Religious, VII-169 pp., 1935.
99. Whalen, Rev. Donald W., A.M., J.C.D., The Value of Testimonial Evidence in Matrimonial Procedure, XIII-297 pp., 1935.
100. Cleary, Rev. Joseph F., J.C.D., Canonical Limitations on the Alienation of Church Property, VIII-141 pp., 1936.
101. Glynn, Rev. John C., J.C.D., The Promoter of Justice, XX-337 pp., 1936.
102. Brennan, Rev. James H., S.S., M.A., S.T.B., J.C.D., The Simple Convalidation of Marriage, VI-135 pp., 1937.
103. Bunini, Rev. Joseph Bernard, J.C.D., The Clerical Obligations of Canons 139 and 142, X-121 pp., 1937.
104. Connor, Rev. Maurice, A.B., J.C.D,. The Administrative Removal of Pastors, VIII-159 pp., 1937.
105. Guilfoyle, Rev. Merlin Joseph, J.C.D., Custom, XI-144 pp., 1937.
106. Hughes, Rev. James Austin, A.B., A.M., J.C.D., Witnesses in Criminal Trials of Clerics, IX-140 pp., 1937.
107. Jansen, Rev. Raymond J., A.B., S.T.L., J.C.D., Canonical Provisions for Catechetical Instruction, VII-153 pp., 1937.
108. Kealy, Rev. John James, A.B., J.C.D., The Introductory Libellus in Church Court Procedure, XI-121 pp., 1937.
109. McManus, Rev. James Edward, C.SS.R., J.C.D., The Administration of Temporal Goods in Religious Institutes, XVI-196 pp., 1937.
110. Moriarty, Rev. Eugene James, J.C.D., Oaths in Ecclesiastical Courts, X-115 pp., 1937.
111. Rainer, Rev. Eligius George, C.SS.R., J.C.D., Suspension of Clerics, XVII-249 pp., 1937.
112. Reilly, Rev. Thomas F., C.SS.R., J.C.D., Visitation of Religious, VI-195 pp., 1938.
113. Moriarity, Rev. Francis E., C.SS.R., J.C.D., The Extraordinary Absolution from Censures, XV-334 pp., 1938.
114. Connolly, Rev. Nicholas P., J.C.D., The Canonical Erection of Parishes, X-132 pp., 1938.
115. Donovan, Rev. James Joseph, J.C.D., The Pastor's Obligation in Prenuptial Investigation, XII-322 pp., 1938.

116. Harrigan, Rev. Robert J., M.A., S.T.B., J.C.D., The Radical Sanation of Invalid Marriages, XII-236 pp., 1939.
117. Boffa, Rev. Conrad Humbert, J.C.D., Canonical Provisions for Catholic Schools, VII-211 pp., 1939.
118. Parsons, Rev. Anscar John, O.M.Cap., J.C.D., Canonical Elections,XII-236 pp., 1939.
119. Reilly, Rev. Edward Michael, A.B., J.C.D., The General Norms of Dispensation, XII-156 pp., 1939.
120. Ryan, Rev. Gerald Aloysius, A.B., J.C.D., Principles of Episcopal Jurisdiction, XII-172 pp., 1939.
121. Burton, Rev. Francis James, C.S.C., A.B., J.C.D. A Commentary on Canon 1125, X-222 pp., 1940.
122. Miaskiewicz, Rev. Francis Sigismund, J.C.D., Supplied Jurisdiction According to Canon 209, XII-340 pp., 1940.
123. Rice, Rev. Patrick William, A.B., J.C.D., Proof of Death in Prenuptial Investigation, VIII-156 pp., 1940.
124. Anglin, Rev. Thomas Francis, M.S., J.C.D., The Eucharistic Fast, VIII-183 pp., 1941.
125. Coleman, Rev. John Jerome, J.C.D., The Minister of Confirmation, VI-153 pp., 1941.
126. Downs, Rev. Joseph Emmanuel, A.B., J.C.D., The Concept of Clerical Immunity, XI-163 pp., 1941.
127. Esswein, Rev. Anthony Albert, J.C.D., Extrajudicial Penal Powers of Ecclesiastical Superiors, X-144 pp., 1941.
128. Farrell, Rev. Benjamin Francis, M.A., S.T.L., J.C.D., The Rights and Duties of the Local Ordinary Regarding Congregations of Women Religious of Pontifical Approval, V-195 pp., 1941.
129. Feeney, Rev. Thomas John, A.B., S.T.L., J.C.D., Restitutio in Integrum, VI-169 pp., 1941.
130. Findlay, Rev. Stephen William, O.S.B., A.B., J.C.D., Canonical Norms Governing the Deposition and Degradation of Clerics, XVII-279 pp., 1941.
131. Goodwine, Rev. John, A.B., S.T.L., J.C.D., The Right of the Church to Acquire Property, VIII-119 pp., 1941.
132. Heston, Rev. Edward Louis, C.S.C., Ph.D., S.T.D., J.C.D., The Alienation of Church Property in the United States, XII-222 pp., 1941.
133. Hogan, Rev. James John, A.B., S.T.L., J.C.D., Judicial Advocates and Procurators, XIII-200 pp., 1941.
134. Kealy, Rev. Thomas M., A.B., Litt.D., J.C.D., Dowry of Women Religious, IX-152 pp., 1941.
135. Keene, Rev. Michael James, O.S.B., J.C.D., Religious Ordinaries and Canon 198, V-164 pp., 1942.
136. Kebin, Rev. Charles A., S.S., M.A., S.T.B., J.C.D., The Privation of Christian Burial, XVI-279 pp., 1941.
137. Louis, Rev. William Francis, M.A., J.C.D., Diocesan Archives, X-101 pp., 1941.
138. McDevitt, Rev. Gilbert Joseph, A.B., J.C.D., Legitimacy and Legitimation, X-247 pp., 1941.

139. McDonough, Rev. Thomas Joseph, A.B., J.C.D., Apostolic Administrators, X-217 pp., 1941.
140. Meier, Rev. Carl Anthony, A.B., J.C.D., Penal Administration Procedure Against Negligent Pastors, XI-240 pp., 1941.
141. Schmidt, Rev. John Rogg, A.B., J.C.D., The Principles of Authentic Interpretation in Canon 17 of the Code of Canon Law, XII-331 pp., 1941.
142. Slafkosky, Rev. Andrew Leonard, A.B., J.C.D., The Canonical Episcopal Visitation of the Diocese, X-197 pp., 1941.
143. Swoboda, Rev. Innocent Robert, O.F.M., J.C.D., Ignorance in Relation to the Imputability of Delicts, IX-271 pp., 1941.
144. Dube, Rev. Arthur Joseph, A.B., J.C.D., The General Principles for the Reckoning of Time in Canon Law, VIII-299 pp., 1941.
145. McBride, Rev. James T., A.B., J.C.D., Incardination and Excardination of Seculars, XX-585 pp., 1941.
146. Krol, Rev. John T., J.C.D., The Defendant in Ecclesiastical Trials, XII-207 pp., 1942.
147. Comyns, Rev. Joseph J., C.SS.R., A.B., J.C.D., Papal and Episcopal Administration of Church Property, XIV-155 pp., 1942.
148. Barry, Rev. Garrett Francis, O.M.I., J.C.D., Violation of the Cloister, XII-260 pp., 1942.
149. Bolduc, Rev. Gatien, C.S.V., A.B., S.T.L., J.C.D., Les Etudes dans les Religions Cléricales, VIII-155 pp., 1942.
150. Boyle, Rev. David John, M.A., J.C.D., The Juridic Effects of Moral Certitude on Pre-Nuptial Guarantees, XII-188 pp., 1942.
151. Canavan, Rev. Walter Joseph, M.A., Litt.D., J.C.D., The Profession of Faith, XII-143 pp., 1942.
152. Desrochers, Rev. Bruno, A.B., Ph.L., S.T.B., J.C.D., Le Premier Concile Plénier de Québec et le Code de Droit Canonique, XIV-186 pp., 1942.
153. Dillon, Rev. Robert Edward, A.B., J.C.D., Common Law Marriage, X-148 pp., 1942.
154. Dodwell, Rev. Edward John, Ph.D., S.T.B., J.C.D., The Time and Place for the Celebration of Marriage, X-156 pp., 1942.
155. Donnellan, Rev. Thomas Andrew, A.B., J.C.D., The Obligation of the Missa pro Populo, VII-131 pp., 1942.
156. Eltz, Rev. Louis Anthony, A.B., J.C.L., Cooperation in Crime.
157. Gass, Rev. Sylvester Francis, M.A., J.C.D., Ecclesiastical Pensions, XI-206 pp., 1942.
158. Guiniven, Rev. John Joseph, C.SS.R., J.C.D. ,The Precept of Hearing Mass, XIV-188 pp., 1942.
159. Gulczynski, Rev. John Theophilus, J.C.D., The Desecration and Violation of Churches, X-126 pp., 1942.
160. Hammill, Rev. John Leo, M.A. J.C.D., The Obligations of the Traveler According to Canon 14, VIII-204 pp., 1942.
161. Haydt, Rev. John Joseph, A.B., J.C.D., Reserved Benefices, XI-148 pp., 1942.
162. Huber, Rev. Roger John, O.F.M., A.B., J.C.D., The Crime of Abortion in Canon Law, XII-187 pp., 1942.

163. Kearney, Rev. Francis Patrick, A.B., S.T.L., J.C.L., The Principles of Canon 1127.

164. Linahen, Rev. Leo James, S.T.L., J.C.D., De Absolutione Complicis In Peccato Turpi, 114 pp., 1942.

165. McCloskey, Rev. Joseph Aloysius, A.B., J.C.D., The Subject of Ecclesiastical Law According to Canon 12, XVII-246 pp., 1942.

166. O'Neill, Rev. Francis Joseph, C.SS.R., J.C.D., The Dismissal of Religious in Temporary Vows, XIII-220 pp., 1942.

167. Prince, Rev. John Edward, A.B., S.T.D., J.C.D., The Diocesan Chancellor, X-136 pp., 1942.

168. Riesner, Rev. Albert Joseph, C.SS.R., J.C.D., Apostates and Fugitives from Religious Institutes, IX-168 pp., 1942.

169. Stenger, Rev. Joseph Bernard, J.C.D., The Mortgaging of Church Property, 186 pp., 1942.

170. Waldron, Rev. Joseph Francis, A.B., J.C.D., The Minister of Baptism, XII-197 pp., 1942.

171. Willett, Rev. Robert Albert, J.C.D., The Probative Value of Documents in Ecclesiastical Trials, X-124 pp., 1942.

172. Woeber, Rev. Edward Martin, M.A., J.C.D., The Interpellations, XII-161 pp., 1942.

173. Benko, Rev. Matthew Aloysius, O.S.B., M.A., J.C.L., The Abbot *Nullius*.

174. Christ, Rev. Joseph James, M.A., S.T.L., J.C.L., Dispensation from Vindicative Penalties.

175. Clancy, Rev. Patrick M. J., O.P., A.B., S.T.Lr., J.C.D., The Local Religious Superior, X-299 pp., 1943.

176. Clarke, Rev. Thomas James, J.C.D., Parish Societies, XII-147 pp., 1943.

177. Connolly, Rev. John Patrick, S.T.L., J.C.D., Synodal Examiners and Parish Priest Consultors, X-223 pp., 1943.

178. Drumm, Rev. William Martin, A.B., J.C.L., Hospital Chaplains.

179. Flanagan, Rev. Bernard Joseph, A.B., S.T.L., J.C.D., The Canonical Erection of Religious Houses, X-147 pp., 1943.

180. Kelleher, Rev. Stephen Joseph, A.B., S.T.B., J.C.D., Discussions with non-Catholics: Canonical Legislation, X-93 pp., 1943.

181. Lewis, Rev. Gordian, C.P., J.C.D., Chapters in Religious Institutes, XII-169 pp., 1943.

182. Marx, Rev. Adolph, J.C.D., The Declaration of Nullity of Marriages Contracted Outside the Church, X-151 pp., 1943.

183. Matulenas, Rev. Raymond Anthony, O.S.B., A.B., J.C.L., Communication, a Source of Privileges.

184. O'Leary, Rev. Charles Gerard, C.SS.R., J.C.D., Religious Dismissed After Perpetual Profession, X-213 pp., 1943.

185. Power, Rev. Cornelius Michael, J.C.L., The Blessing of Cemeteries.

186. Shuhler, Rev. Ralph Vincent, O.S.A., J.C.D., Privileges of Regulars to Absolve and Dispense, XII-195 pp., 1943.

187. Ziolkowski, Rev. Thaddeus Stanislaus, A.B., J.C.D., The Consecration and Blessing of Churches, XII-151 pp., 1943.

188. HENEGHAN, REV. JOHN JOSEPH, S.T.D., J.C.L., The Marriages of Unworthy Catholics: Canons 1065 and 1066, XVI-213 pp., 1944.
189. CARROLL, REV. COLEMAN FRANCIS, M.A., S.T.L., J.C.L., Charitable Institutions.
190. CIESLUK, REV. JOSEPH EDWARD, Ph.B., S.T.L., J.C.L., National Parishes in the United States, VI-178 pp., 1944.
191. COBURN, REV. VINCENT PAUL, A.B., J.C.L., Marriages of Conscience. XII-172 pp., 1944.
192. CONNORS, REV. CHARLES PAUL, C.S.Sp., A.B., J.C.L., Extra-Judicial Procurators in the Code of Canon Law, X-94 pp., 1944.
193. COYLE, REV. PAUL RAYMOND, A.B., J.C.L., Judicial Exceptions. pp., 1944.
194. FAIR, REV. BARTHOLOMEW FRANCIS, A.B., S.T.L., J.C.L., The Impediment of Abduction, XII-122 pp., 1944.
195. GALLAGHER, REV. THOMAS RAPHAEL, O.P., A.B., S.T.Lr., J.C.L., The Examination of the Qualities of the Ordinand, X-166 pp., 1944.
196. GANNON, REV. JOHN MARK, S.T.L., J.C.L., The Interstices Required for the Promotion to orders, XII-100 pp., 1944.
197. GOLDSMITH, REV. J. WILLIAM, B.C.S., S.T.L., J.C.L., The Competence of Church and State over Marriage—Disputed Points, X-128 pp., 1944.
198. GOODWINE, REV. JOSEPH GERARD, A.B., S.T.B., J.C.L., The Reception of Converts, XIV-326 pp., 1944.
199. KOWALSKI, REV. ROMUALD, EUGENE, O.F.M., A.B., J.C.L., Sustenance of Religious Houses of Regulars, X-174 pp., 1944.
200. McCOY, REV. ALAN EDWARD, O.F.M., J.C.L., Force and Fear in Relation to Delictual Imputability and Penal Responsibility, XII-160 pp., 1944.
201. McDEVITT, REV. VINCENT JOHN, Ph.B., S.T.L., J.C.L., Perjury.
202. MARTIN, REV. THOMAS OWEN, Ph.D., S.T.D., J.C.L., Adverse Possession, Prescription and Limitation of Actions: The Canonical "Praescriptio," XX-208 pp., 1944.
203. MIKLOSOVIC, REV. PAUL JOHN, A.B., J.C.L., Attempted Marriages and Their Consequent Juridic Effects.
204. MUNDY, REV. THOMAS MAURICE, A.B., S.T.L., J.C.L., The Union of Parishes, X-164 pp., 1944.
205. O'DEA, REV. JOHN COYLE, A.B., J.C.L., The Matrimonial Impediment of Nonage, VII-126 pp., 1944.
206. OLALIA, REV. ALEXANDER AYSON, S.T.L., J.C.L., A Comparative Study of the Christian Constitution of States and the Constitution of the Philippine Commonwealth, XII-136 pp., 1944.
207. POISSON, REV. PIERRE-MARIE, C.S.C., A.B., Ph.L., Th.L., J.C.L., Droits Patrimoniaux des Maisons et des Eglises Religieuses.
208. STADALNIKAS, REV. CASIMIR JOSEPH, M.I.C., J.C.L., Reservation of Censures, X-141 pp., 1944.
209. SULLIVAN, REV. EUGENE HENRY, S.T.L., J.C.L., Proof of the Reception of the Sacraments, X-165 pp., 1944.
210. VAUGHAN, REV. WILLIAM EDWARD, J.C.L., Constitutions for Diocesan Courts, X-210 pp., 1944.
211. PARO, REV. GINO, S.T.D., J.C.L., The Right of Apostolic Legation.
212. BALZER, REV. RALPH FRANCIS, C.P., J.C.L., The Computation of Time in a Canonical Novitiate, X-227 pp., 1945.

213. Dougherty, Rev. John Whelan, A.B., S.T.L., J.C.L., De Inquisitione Speciali, XII-195 pp., 1945.
214. Dziob, Rev. Michael Walter, J.C.L., The Sacred Congregation for the Oriental Church.
215. Eidenschink, Rev. John Albert, O.S.B., B.A., J.C.L., The Election of Bishops in the Letters of Pope Gregory the Great.
216. Gill, Rev. Nicholas, C.P., J.C.L., The Spiritual Prefect in Clerical Religious Houses of Study.
217. Hynes, Rev. Harry Gerard, S.T.L., J.C.D., The Privileges of Cardinals, XII-183 pp., 1945.
218. McDevitt, Rev. Gerard Vincent, S.T.L., J.C.D., The Renunciation of an Ecclesiastical Office, XIV—179 pp., 1946.
219. Manning, Rev. Joseph Leroy, J.C.L., The Free Conferral of Offices.
220. Meyer, Rev. Louis G., O.S.B., A.B., S.T.B., J.C.D., Alms-Gathering by Religious, XII—163 pp., 1946.
221. O'Donnell, Rev. Cletus Francis, M.A., J.C.D., The Marriage of Minors, XII-268 pp., 1945.
222. Prunskis, Rev. Joseph, J.C.D., Comparative Law, Ecclesiastical and Civil, in Lithuanian Concordat, X-161 pp., 1945.
223. Sweeney, Rev. Francis Patrick, C.SS.R., J.C.D., The Reduction of Clerics to the Lay State, X-199 pp., 1945.
224. Vogelpohl, Rev. Henry John, J.C.D., The Simple Impediments to Holy Orders, XVI-190 pp., 1945.
225. Brockhaus, Rev. Thomas Aquinas, O.S.B., J.C.D., Religious Who Are Known as *Conversi*, X-127 pp., 1945.
226. Griese, Rev. N. Orville, S.T.D., J.C.D., The Marriage Contract and the Procreation of Offspring, XVI-224 pp., 1946.
227. Boudreaux, Rev. Warren Louis, J.C.D., The "*ab acatholicis nati*" of Canon 1099, § 2, XII-110 pp., 1946.
228. Bowe, Rev. Thomas Joseph, A.B., J.C.D., Religious Superioresses, VIII-206 pp., 1946.
229. Diederichs, Rev. Michael Ferdinand, S.C.J., J.C.D., The Jurisdiction of the Latin Ordinaries Over Their Oriental Subjects, XIV-153 pp., 1946.
230. Dingman, Rev. Maurice John, A.B., S.T.L. J.C.L., The Plaintiff in Contentious Trials.
231. Frison, Rev. Basil, C.M.F., M.Mus., J.C.D., The Retroactivity of Law, X-221 pp., 1946.
232. Galvin, Rev. William Anthony, M.A., J.C.D., The Administrative Transfer of Pastors, X11-288 pp., 1946.
233. Goracy, Rev. Joseph C., J.C.L., The Diriment Matrimonial Impediment of Major Orders.
234. Hale, Rev. Joseph Francis, M.A., S.T.L., J.C.L., The Pastor of Burial.
235. Henry, Rev. Joseph Arthur, A.B., J.C.D., The Mass and Holy Communion: Inter-Ritual Law, XII-138 pp., 1946.
236. Linenberger, Rev. Herbert, C.PP.S., J.C.L., The False Denunciation of an Innocent Confessor.
237. Lowry, Rev. James Martin, A.B., J.C.D., Dispensation from Private Vows, XII-266 pp., 1946.

238. Lynch, Rev. George Edward, A.B., S.T.L., J.C.D., Coadjutors and Auxiliaries of Bishops, X-107 pp., 1947.

239. Lynch, Rev. Timothy, M.S.SS.T., J.C.D., Contracts Between Bishops and Religious Congregations, XIV-232 pp., 1946.

240. McClunn, Rev. Justin David, A.B., S.T.L., J.C.D., Administrative Recourse, VII-142 pp., 1946.

241. Lohmuller, Rev. Martin Nicholas, A.B., J.C.D., The Promulgation of Law, XII-140 pp., 1947.

242. McGrath, Rev. James, A.B., J.C.D., The Privilege of the Canon, XII-156 pp., 1946.

243. Marbach, Rev. Joseph Francis, A.B., J.C.D., Marriage Legislation for the Catholics of the Oriental Rites in the United States and Canada, XIV-314 pp., 1946.

244. Shimkus, Rev. Bernard Aloysius, A.B., J.C.L., The Determination and Transfer of Rite.

245. Smith, Rev. Vincent Michael, A.B., S.T.L., J.C.L., Ignorance Affecting Matrimonial Consent.

246. Wachtrle, Rev. Paul Anthony, A.B., J.C.L., The Baptism of the Children of Non-Catholics.

247. Crotty, Rev. Matthew Michael, J.C.D., The Recipient of First Holy Communion, X-142 pp., 1947.

248. Eagleton, Rev. George, J.C.L., The Quinquennial Faculties, Formula IV.

249. Gibbons, Rev. Marion Leo, C.M., LL.B., J.C.D., Domicile of the Wife Unlawfully Separated from Her Husband, XIV-171 pp., 1947.

250. Kelly, Rev. Bernard Matthew, S.T.L., J.C.D., The Functions Reserved to Pastors, XII-141 pp., 1947.

251. Kilcullen, Rev. Thomas John, LL.M., J.C.D., The Collegiate Moral Person as Party Litigant, X-150 pp., 1947.

252. Lafontaine, Rev. Germain Joseph, W.F., J.C.L., Relations Canoniques entre le Missionnaire et Ses Superieurs.

253. Lane, Rev. Loras Thomas, A.B., S.T.L., J.C.L., Matrimonial Procedure in the Ordinary Court of Second Instance.

254. Lover, Rev. James Francis, C.SS.R., J.C.D., The Master of Novices, X-168 pp., 1947.

255. McNicholas, Rev. Timothy Joseph, J.C.L., The *Septimae Manus* Witness.

256. Marositz, Rev. Joseph John, M.S.C., J.C.D., Obligations and Privileges of Religious Promoted to the Episcopal or Cardinalatial Dignities, XII-180 pp., 1947.

257. Murphy, Rev. Francis Joseph, A.B., J.C.D., Legislative Powers of the Provincial Council, XII-158 pp., 1947.

258. O'Brien, Rev. Romaeus William, O.Carm., J.C.D., The Provincial Superior in Religious Orders of Men, X-294 pp., 1947.

259. Pfaller, Rev. Benedict Augustine, O.S.B., J.C.L., The *Ipso Facto* Effected Dismissal of Religious.

260. Popek, Rev. Alphonse Sylvester, M.A., J.C.D., The Rights and Obligations of Metropolitans, XVIII-460 pp., 1947

261. RISTUCCIA, REV. BERNARD JOSEPH, C.M., J.C.L., Quasi-Religious.
262. SONNTAG, REV. NATHANIEL LOUIS, O.F.M.CAP., J.C.D., Censorship of Special Classes of Books, XII-147 pp., 1947.
263. STADLER, REV. JOSEPH NICHOLAS, J.C.L., Frequent Holy Communion.
264. SZAL, REV. IGNATIUS JOSEPH, J.C.L., The Communication of Catholics with Schismatics.
265. WAGNER, REV. URBAN STANLEY, O.F.M.CONV., J.C.D., Parochial Substitute Vicars and Supplying Priests, X-126 pp., 1947.
266. QUINN, REV. JOSEPH, M.A., J.C.L., Documents Required for the Reception of Orders.
267. BENNINGTON, REV. JAMES CLEMENT, A.B., J.C.L., The Recipient of Confirmation.
268. BLAHER, REV. DAMIAN JOSEPH, O.F.M., A.B., J.C.L., The Ordinary Processes in Causes of Beatification and Canonization.
269. CLUNE, REV. ROBERT BELL, B.A., J.C.L. Judicial Interrogation of the Parties.
270. COURTEMANCHE, REV. BASIL F., B.A., J.C.L., The Total Simulation of Matrimonial Consent.
271. DLOUHY, REV. MAUR JOHN, O.S.B. A,B., J.C.L., The Ordination of Exempt Religious.
272. DONOVAN, REV. JOHN THOMAS, PH.B., S.T.L., J.C.L., The Clerical Obligations of Canons 138 and 140.
273. FREKING, REV. FREDERICK W., A.B., S.T.B., J.C.L., The Canonical Installation of Pastors.
274. FULTON, REV. THOMAS B., J.C.L., Prenuptial Investigation.
275. GODLEY, REV. JAMES P., J.C.L. The Time and the Place for the Celebration of Mass.
276. KANE, REV. THOMAS A., A.B., B.S., J.C.L., Jurisdiction of Patriarchs until 1439.
277. KENNEDY, REV. ANDREW A., J.C.L., The Annual Pastoral Report to the Local Ordinary.
278. KONRAD, REV. JOSEPH GEORGE, J.C.L., Transfer of Religious.
279. KRESS, REV. ALPHONSE, J.C.L., Contumacy in Ecclesiastical Trials.
280. MCCARTNEY, REV. MARCELLUS ANTHONY, O.F.M., M.A., J.C.L., Faculties of Regular Confessors.
281. MCCASLIN, REV. EDWARD PATRICK, M.A., S.T.L., J.C.L., The Division of Parishes.
282. MCELROY, REV. FRANCIS J., A.B., J.C.L., The Privileges of Bishops.
283. QUINN, REV. STEPHEN, M.S.SS.T., J.C.L., Relation between the Local Ordinary and Religious of Diocesan Approval.
284. SCHNEIDER, REV. EDELHARD LOUIS, S.D.S., M.A., J.C.L., The Status of Secularized Ex-Religious Clerics.
285. THOMPSON, REV. CHESTER J., A.B., J.C.L., The Simple Removal from Office.

www.ingramcontent.com/pod-product-compliance
Lightning Source LLC
LaVergne TN
LVHW050209080826
844660LV00012B/386

* 9 7 8 0 8 1 3 2 2 4 4 8 0 *